THE BOY WHO FEARED HIS OWN REFLECTION

AN INTROVERT'S JOURNEY
BOOK 1

LIAM BELLAMY

Illustrated by J E LARSON

Illustrated by ANASTASIA SOROKA

Edited by KATHY WAGHORN

CONTENTS

PROLOGUE

I've always wondered—do other people find it hard to talk? Like there's an invisible force field stopping words from escaping your mouth. Some are naturals at it. They can talk as if it were an Olympic sport. *Am I the only one?*

With these thoughts swirling around and pooling in my brain, I turned my head towards the star-strewn ceiling above.

I smiled a little as I remembered how hard Dad had worked on my room. He painted the whole solar system on the ceiling, complete with glow-in-the-dark stars. The main light was decorated to look like the Sun.

I often imagined what it would feel like to live in outer space. Do planets have feelings too? **Jupiter**, that giant swirling ball of gases and liquids. It must feel reassuring, knowing that no nosey astronauts could ever land on its surface. And then there's **Mercury**, how does it feel being beaten up by meteorites? Imagine having a constant headache, each impact ringing through your rocky insides. But I feel most for **Pluto.** Too small to be taken seriously, too distant to belong. Does it feel lonely, drifting in the icy abyss? Poor Pluto, forever on the outside.

No, perhaps it's not so easy up there.

My name is William, by the way, but I prefer Will. We lived far away from the centre of town in our little semi-detached house on the corner of Oak Street. It was nestled amongst the trees and green pastures of the countryside. So, there wasn't much light outside.

I peered out my bedroom window. Just beyond the garden, over the Dower hills, huge swathes of farmland stretched as far as the eye could see. There was a barn in the field closest to us. It was an old, creaky patchwork of wood, nothing special. But every night I went over to my telescope and observed it. I saw the faint glow of a light coming from inside. And every time that light flickered, I could just make out something ginormous inside. It was too big to be a tractor or farming machinery. It was hidden, a large tarp sheet draped over it. A man—I guessed was the farmer—would go in there every night.

My entire body would shiver at the thought that he might catch me at any moment. Sometimes I would hear horrifying screeching noises, like an animal in pain, and when I scrambled out of bed to see what had made the noise, the light had already disappeared, and the farmer walked out with his two burly dogs by his side.

I wanted to find out what secrets were hiding in that barn. No, I *needed* to. My curiosity was too strong, and the need for answers overpowered all logic, all of which pointed to DANGER!

But another voice began whispering in my ear. A voice that told every inch of my body to fear the unknown, to get away from it. I had a name for this wicked voice, but I fear that if I say it again, they might return.

1

THE BEAST IN THE WOODS

I was stuck at Barnsmead Park Primary School. It was an old school, and it seemed as though nothing had changed since it opened in the seventies. I saw the cyan-coloured paint chips peeling off the walls, the tattered moth-ridden curtains, the smeared chalk-stained blackboards.

It was the beginning of a new school year. In fact, it was Year 6, the final year of primary school, and I was already itching to leave. I wouldn't miss this place. Not one bit.

Changes were happening. Relationships were forming, cliques were branching off, and owning rare trading cards was the height of currency.

Autumn was creeping in, and summer was fading away, the leaves had already turned crispy and stale. Summer didn't last long here. It was lunch time, and my best friend Tony was sick that day, so I wandered around the playground by myself. I was extremely aware of the students playing around me with all their friends. I would often pull this trick where I squinted and scanned the playground aimlessly so it looked like I was trying to find my imaginary group of friends. A crinkled leaf blew past my face, and landed next to a small, wooded area in the corner of the playing field. My attention became fixed on the swaying branches and creaking tree trunks. I stared at it for a great amount of time. I stared for so long that people eventually disappeared. The students' hysterical laughter and chatter became muffled and gently fell away. The only sign of movement and sound came from within the murky woods.

It was as though something was calling to me.

The leaves brushed against one another, scraping and scratching. I took a huge inhale, readying myself. I knew I'd have to investigate this oddity alone.

I cautiously took the first steps towards the mysterious woods. My freshly waxed school shoes grazed the grass that gradually reached knee-height. The harsh sounds of the dying plants became louder. The trees revealed a narrow gateway where one small human could have entered if they squeezed themselves through the gap. Looking deep into the heart of the woods revealed nothing but sheer darkness. I trembled with fearful excitement.

In a weird way, I think I enjoyed the fear—the mystery of it all.

I took a step through the entrance. My shoes met with the unmistakable squelch of wet mud. I was too curious to care about what Mum would think; that was a problem to deal with later. There was a rustle in the trees up ahead. A morbid thought crept across my mind. *I'm going to die.*

THRASH!

I leapt backwards. A couple of pigeons scattered, disturbing the trees as they flew away. *Phew. Pigeons. Just pigeons.*

I'd had enough of the cave of horrors. The school bell droned in the distance. It was time to head back.

Just as I turned around, I heard a *crunch*. I lifted my shoe, but there were no leaves underneath. A sharp, needle-piercing feeling stabbed my entire body. An icy grip latched onto my arms and feet, locking them in place, as though held by invisible chains. I could just barely manage to turn my head.

Beyond the dark abyss, a tall silhouette approached. Its footsteps thudded and shook the ground. It reached a sliver of light poking through the canopy. The light barely revealed its identity, but it was enough. It was at least eight feet tall. A monstrosity with huge, lifeless black eyes, protruding walrus-like tusks, and a face covered in brown matted fur. It made a guttural sound, like a running engine, as it approached.

When you watch a movie, usually the victim screams, but I made no sound; I was incapable. Instead, I ran. The grass seemed thicker than before as I awkwardly waded through it. It felt as though bricks were weighing me down, and the safety of the school building didn't feel any closer. My legs heaved with all their might to lift off the ground. I dared not glance back at the beast, but I couldn't help taking one final look. All I saw was a blur of mushy browns and smeared greens. I tripped clumsily over my shoelaces and landed on the muddy ground. I craned my head up to see another monstrosity. *Mrs Collings!*

She was standing over me, hand on hip. I never thought I'd be so relieved to see her glum face.

'Late. Again,' she snapped.

I wanted to say something, warn her of the danger lurking in the woods, but I knew she wouldn't believe me.

'And look at your shoes!' she bellowed.

2

THE CLASS FROM HELL

I couldn't help but think about that monstrous, lanky mountain of hair and teeth as I followed Mrs Collings back to the classroom, tail between my legs. I was sure it was real. I'd felt its rancid breath, seen the buzzing of the flies that circled its head, the hot steam it blew from its nostrils. It was real ... wasn't it?

The bell cried out. The sound startled me.

'Find a seat,' Mrs Collings said nonchalantly.

She was our class teacher. I would estimate she was around fifty. She was also our maths teacher, so I figured she knew everything.

The classroom desks were huddled close together, and I hated wriggling through them, causing any unwanted attention. Everyone had already partnered up, their desks pushed together like they were married couples. I lost out on the seating arrangement lottery. The cool kids secured the desks at the back, where they could remain undetected whilst they flicked wet paper at the unlucky student in front. I had a lovely place right in the front and centre of the room. Hurray.

I plopped myself down and peered up at the massive blackboard. The word *ICEBREAKER* was boldly scribbled on it.

Oh no, I thought. I had heard of *ice* and *break* before, and they certainly didn't sound like positive words.

Mrs Collings paused and studied the room. 'I want you to think of one interesting fact about yourself, then share it with the class.'

That same sensation returned in an instant. A sharp pain punctured my stomach. My face became numb and frozen. *Wh ... What is this?* I knew something was wrong. I looked to my left to check if another student had shanked me with a pencil. No, this was something else.

'So, any volunteers?' she asked. Nobody answered. Mrs Collings rolled her eyes. 'OK, I'll pick someone.'

My adrenaline shot up. My eyes darted around the room to calculate my odds of being chosen. *So, there's a one in sixteen chance. If I divide by four ... wait, what's divide again? OK. OK. If I put my head down, she probably won't see—*

'William, isn't it? Come on, tell us your interesting fact.'

My eyes glazed over. There was a silence in the room that was hard to describe. You know those rooms with sound-proofing walls that are so quiet you can hear the blood moving through your veins? Yeah, kind of like that.

'I ... like. Interesting ...' My palms were sweaty, and I couldn't even look to see, but I was sure my classmates' eyes were glued to me.

CRACK!

A horrendous heaving of the ground broke the class-room apart. My desk began slipping into the growing chasm below. My attention was diverted from the teacher, and my eyes widened as I stared beneath my feet to witness flames lapping at my ankles. I clamoured on top of the desk to steady myself. Mrs Collings's stony face transformed into a menacing smile. Her eyes grew three times bigger; the fire reflected and danced in her pupils as she let out a truly wicked laugh. *HAHAHAHA. You're probably the most boring student I've ever taught!*

She was towering over me as I sank lower into the fiery pit.

Quick, say something, I desperately pleaded to myself. *Anything. Say anything.*

The sound of the students laughing joined in the cacophony of sound. The piercing echoes rang and pinged off the walls directly into my ears.

What's wrong with him?

He's weird.

I clasped my hands over my ears, attempting to block out all senses. It was useless. More chattering students joined in.

Maybe there's nothing interesting about him.

This was the end. I was going to sink into oblivion unless I said something right then.

'I ... I ... I like space,' I said.

Crickets.

The whispering and raging fires vanished. I looked down—the floor was intact. It was filthy but otherwise completely ordinary. I looked up at Mrs Collings. Her eyes were normal-sized, and she wasn't laughing. Instead, she had a sympathetic, slightly upwardly curled smile.

'Space, yeah. That's good. Interesting. OK, does anyone else want to try? I don't want to pick on anyone ...'

She trailed off, and my thoughts turned inward again. *What was* that?

I observed the room, and not a single student was

looking in my direction. Did they care? Did they notice me? It was not something I could begin to process, but I knew something was wrong. This didn't feel 'normal'.

But I didn't know what 'normal' was.

3

IT

Tony came back to school after a week of illness. He'd had chickenpox. One of the certainties of being a kid is getting these itchy sores all over your body. But you get to play video games all week while being spoon-fed licorice-flavoured medicine. Not a bad trade.

Tony was my best friend. He came to school in Year 3, and because I was assigned to show him around, we quickly got along. He was big for his age, stocky, buzzed black hair against glistening blue eyes. He was odd, hyperactive, but seemed to enjoy my strange sense of humour, and I enjoyed his frantic energy.

We were sitting in the computer suite. It was our first IT lesson, and we were so excited to be taught how to use the computers. Tony didn't care much about the boring technical stuff, he just wanted to know how to install the latest football game.

'Hey, did you get chickenpox already?' Tony whispered to me.

'Yeah, I had it like three years ago,' I whispered back.

'Did you give it me?'

'What? No. I don't think it works like that!' I said.

'Oh. OK. Did Charlene say anything when I was sick?' He looked over at her not-so-discreetly.

I knew Tony had a thing for her. She was one of the most popular students in the year. She was kind and treated everyone equally. All the boys liked her.

'Charlene?' I asked, pretending to mishear him. 'No, I don't think she said anything.'

'Well, maybe because she doesn't talk to you? Maybe she said something to her friends.'

As sound as Tony's logic was, it still hurt to hear that.

'Yeah, maybe.' I sighed.

Tony turned his attention to the teacher.

I tilted my chair back slightly and glanced over at Charlene talking with her friend, giggling about something. She had light auburn brown hair and cute freckles covering her face like polka dots. I wanted to say something, anything to get her attention. But my mouth felt as though it was filled with concrete. So, I just sat there, gawping at her. Her friend made her laugh so loud she snorted a little. It must have been a funny joke because I laughed out loud, really loud, while staring them right in the face. The teacher stopped in his tracks. The whole class swivelled in my direction. Instantly, beads of sweat dripped down my face like a leaky tap.

Charlene whispered something to her friend, and I couldn't bear to look at her again.

'Loser.'

I ducked down under the table as fast as I could.

'Everyone heard you.'

The voices grew louder, but I couldn't tell where they were coming from.

'*Does he like her? That is so sad.*'

'*Why would she even think about him?*'

Without warning, a fierce rage from inside me burst out violently. 'LEAVE ME ALONE!'

The awkward silence had never been so loud before.

Did I just say that out loud? I groaned.

Tony ran over to the microphone connected to the PA system (basically the speakers that play in classrooms over the entire school).

'I love cheese!' he yelled.

He'd created a distraction.

It was enough. Everyone turned and gawked at him. I wondered if he did that to save me from further humiliation or just wanted to do something stupid.

I can't remember the rest of that IT class; I wish I could, but the sheer embarrassment ruined any chance of talking to Charlene again anytime soon.

4

THE MYSTERY

Later that day, Tony and I were jogging around the playground, scheming our next adventure. We first cooked up the idea of investigating UFOs and paranormal activities two years ago today. We would investigate strange phenomena, like objects flying off shelves or seeing famous people on pieces of toast. Our small group of wannabe detectives decided to call ourselves The Mystery, which in hindsight doesn't sound like the most creative name. But we took it one hundred percent seriously.

Our investigations never took us beyond the school gates; there was a terrifying, unknown world beyond it, so the closest we got was touching the cold steely bars, if we dared. Instead, we used the school as our main base of operations.

I decided now would be a good time to mention to Tony what I saw in the barn the other night. I knew he'd be interested too; his curiosity for the unknown almost equally matched mine.

As I ran, the concrete running track was unforgiving on my heels; it was like running on a bed of hot coals.

'I'm pretty sure the farmer is hiding something down my street. We could check it out,' I said through gasps of air.

'Really? What did it look like?' Tony asked.

'I don't know. It's hidden. He's keeping it in the barn.'

His eyes filled with intrigue. 'You think it's alien?'

'What?'

'The thing in the barn!'

We looped around the running track and around the wooden flower crates at each corner. Each passing lap pushed my limits.

'Maybe I could use my telescope to see it closer,' I suggested.

'Nah, we could just go inside and take a look. I bet it's easy.'

'Ha,' I laughed nervously. 'You haven't seen that place. It has metal wire all the way around it.'

Tony picked up the pace. I breathed heavily as I caught up with him.

His brow furrowed. 'Did you actually see anything?'

'Yeah, I did. You weren't even there when I saw—' I cut myself off. *Should I tell him about the walrus-beast I saw in the woods?* I wasn't even sure what I saw.

His impatience grew. 'Huh? What? You saw what?'

'No, it's nothing.'

Tony suddenly changed his line of questioning. 'You ... do you think we should invite Charlene?'

I quickly brushed off the idea. 'Huh? Oh, well, do you really think she'd be interested?'

'I think we should. She's smart, you know? She could be really useful.'

'I don't think that's a good i—'

THUMP!

Tony and I went head over heels and ploughed into the

harsh concrete floor below. I felt the skin on my legs and cheek run over the coarse surface as I ground to a halt. A few drops of crimson-coloured blood dripped onto my white polo shirt.

The two culprits emerged from their cover. Thomas and Dave. I'm not even sure those were their names. The only times I would see them was when they were bullying other children. Did they even attend this school?

It was clear they had stuck their legs out from behind the flower crates to trip us. They didn't show any signs of remorse and instead laughed at us cruelly.

We weakly pulled ourselves upright to look up at the delighted boys.

'Have a nice trip?' They sneered.

My eyes began welling up with tears, but it would be the end of my school career if I cried. I sucked them up.

Thomas and Dave pranced around us, making spooky noises and humming mysterious-sounding music.

'Ooo, something in the barn?' Thomas said, wiggling his fingers.

'Maybe it's a ghost!' Dave added.

'Or a giant dummy.'

They laughed hysterically and made their exit swiftly.

We were left on the cold floor. Tony glanced at me but didn't say anything. I knew he was upset, too, but would never admit it.

He helped pull me to my feet. He sniffed. 'Let's go to the nurse.'

Luckily, no one seemed to have noticed this embarrassing event.

~

IN THE CONFINES of the sterile nurse's office, we sat silently, our legs dangling off the examination table. The air was tinged with alcohol wipes and medical creams. It reminded me of safety and pain at the same time. The nurse tended to our wounds. She dipped a cotton bud in rubbing alcohol and pressed it hard against my cheek. I winced.

'What have you boys been up to, eh?'

I peered over at Tony; he shook his head as if to say, *Don't say a word*.

'Oh, we were just playing. I ran into him, and we just kind of fell over.' I strained the words out. I've never been a natural at lying.

She looked at us suspiciously. 'Hm. Third time you've been here in a month.'

She tended to Tony's wound over his eyebrow. He didn't even flinch.

The nurse finished applying a plaster to my leg. 'Be careful next time,' she said.

～

WE WALKED out into the corridor. Just as we got outside, a girl approached us with a confident stride. She had long blonde pigtails that brushed against her shoulders and a wide, toothy smile. This was Bree. She was a late addition to my small group of friends.

Tony panicked and grabbed me. 'Don't say anything, OK. If you have to lie, say we got hurt playing conkers.'

Bree was already standing two feet away from us. She made direct eye contact with me. I couldn't stand to do the same. I had a problem with eye contact.

'Hey, Bree,' Tony said through a forced fake smile.

'Hi, boys. Wait—' She stopped her sentence short. She

studied the small cuts across our faces. We lowered our heads like two naughty children being scolded by their parents.

'Are you OK?' she asked.

'Who, us?' Tony replied.

'Who else!' She tapped her feet impatiently.

'We're fine. We were playing a game. Conkers. It got pretty crazy.'

She turned her attention on me. Her piercing blue eyes drilled into mine.

'Will? Is that true?'

Tony pinched my arm.

'Ow. I mean, I think so ...' I said, still feeling the sting.

Bree knew I was a bad liar, but she also knew when I wanted to be left alone. She was an eccentric, intelligent girl. She was the responsible one, always arranging and scheduling our adventures. She kept paperwork and tracked all our findings. Without her, Tony and I would be completely lost.

'Hey,' Tony said, perking up. 'Will said he found something in the farmer's field!'

Her eyebrows raised.

I lifted my head. I was glad to be diverted away from that conversation.

'It's in a barn. I'm not sure what it is. But I heard noises.'

'Noises?' she asked.

'Like something was hurt. Or being hurt.'

'Right,' she said. 'We're going. Tomorrow.'

Tony held out his hands and stepped between the two of us. 'Woah. Are you sure you wanna go?' he asked Bree.

'Yeah, duh! We're still a team, aren't we?'

'Of course we are! I just want you to be safe. I think it could be a risky mission.'

'You think I'm not brave?' She sounded hurt.

'What? No, I—'

'Look, boys, sometimes I think you two are mad, but I'm going with you whether you like it or not. I'm still your UFO expert, right?'

'Right,' we confirmed.

'Tomorrow night,' she said.

5

THE REFLECTION

I walked home that afternoon with a slight limp. It was such a decent, harmless town that Mum let me walk home by myself. I didn't mind. I liked the quietness.

It was difficult to walk straight. I was trying to appear as normal as possible. I choked back tears, willing myself to be tougher.

I approached our house on the corner of the street. The windows reflected the sunlight so brightly it was blinding. My injuries were clearly visible, so I quickly hurried inside.

My family moved here when I turned six years old. We originally lived in a run-down area on the outskirts of Mancaster, an almost-city in West Yorkshire. I hated it there.

This house was an improvement over the last one. There weren't any fungi sprouting from between the floorboards, and the walls weren't damp. It was small, but it was home.

'Hellooo,' said Mum in a sing-song voice.

I wanted to dart up to my bedroom so badly. I slipped off my shoes and wriggled off my jacket like a snake shedding its skin. I peered past the reception and into the living room. She wasn't there.

She must be in the kitchen.

I heard the faint sound of pots and pans banging together. My eyes swivelled towards the stairs. At the top awaited my bedroom, door swung open, and a heavenly glow lit up the entrance. Sanctuary.

Before I could move a muscle, my legs began to wobble. *No, really? Now? Why are you doing this now?*

The fear was back, but I couldn't understand why. I was in my own home, usually the base of safety. Nothing could touch me here, so why was I so scared? The stairs began to extend outward into infinity, and the bedroom door violently slammed shut. The angelic light extinguished.

Mum sprung out from the kitchen and bounded towards me. 'Did you have a good day at sc—'

The game was up. She couldn't miss the plasters, the red blotchy skin, the look of worry etched into my face. 'I'm fine,' I muttered, my head bowed.

'Well, I can see that you're not. *This* isn't fine. What happened?'

'I'm fine. Why do you always do this?' I yelled.

I ran up the stairs, burst into my room, and flopped lamely onto the perfectly made bed that awaited me.

I hated those sudden bursts of anger, especially towards people who meant the most to me. I was never *really* angry with them, just deflecting it from those who really deserved it.

Why am I like this? No wonder I have no friends.

With my head buried under the duvet and tears staining the sheets, I knew only one thing could make me forget for a brief period. I pulled out my favourite book from the sacred bookshelf. After straining and forcing my eyes to read the scribbles on the page, the words became blurry, unreadable. It was impossible to concentrate on anything. My mind raced non-stop, synapses firing like electricity dancing between telephone poles.

I'm scared of friendship. I'm terrified of bullies. I'm frightened by my own family. What is wrong with me? Why aren't I like other kids?

I rolled over and stared at the star-strewn ceiling. As I gazed into the light, I noticed the planets started to shift and rotate like a pinwheel. The **Sun** flickered brightly, assaulting my eyes. I stuck out my hands to cover it, but to no use. The gaping void of the universe wrapped around me, under the sheets and around my back until I was completely wrapped in darkness.

I was in outer space.

On my left, **Jupiter** orbited around me—the sheer size was unbelievable. On my right, **Mercury** loomed and bore a dim white glow. I opened my mouth to speak, but I realized there was no oxygen in my lungs; they were useless. I felt something approaching from behind, a presence that felt even darker than the lightless nothingness of space. That familiar icy grip washed over my shoulders. Every hair on my body stood up like a petrified cat.

It's here.

'*What a shame. What a waste,*' said the disembodied voice. Deafening silence fell between its words.

'*This could have been you. Imagine it! You, an astronaut, exploring the unknown regions of the universe.*'

The voice was cool and unwavering. It was so confident in every word it uttered.

I was helplessly drifting through space.

'*All the boys. All of them. They're not scared of talking. Who is? It's just not natural. You see, the ones who trip you up, who make fun of your clothes and your choice of friends, what music you listen to or don't listen to, they've already won. Life will reward them greatly. You're what? Ten years old now? It's already too late for you. This all starts from the beginning— before you can even begin to form a brain. You're born this way, but I understand; you can't help it. An ant can't help being an ant.'*

I listened intently; my eyes forced wide open like there were toothpicks holding up my eyelids.

'You know the polar bear? They're notoriously lonely crea- tures. They choose to live alone. They hunt, feed, sleep, the same routine day after day. You know the difference between you and a polar bear?'

I knew the answer, but I couldn't speak up even if I wanted to. The voice left a long, agonizing pause, taunting me.

'The polar bear isn't scared of anything.'

We were now drifting past **Mars**, which poured out a vivid, crimson red that washed over my entire body. The unnamed entity remained latched around my back and shoulders. I couldn't move.

'I thought it was time I introduced myself. I must admit, it's been a long time coming. I've been hanging around for quite a while now. My name is Phobos.'

He savoured his name as he spoke it.

'It's nice to put a name to the face, yes?'

I suppose from this point I should refer to Phobos as 'them'.

Just like 'Bloody Mary', I would rather not mention their name again, but I wanted to tell you the truth. There shouldn't be any secrets between us.

The stars began to dim, and my body sank back into the bed. My eyes bolted shut. I didn't want Phobos to be real, but somehow, I knew they were.

6

SECRET WINDOW

That terrifying trip to space must have cost me a couple of hours because it was already growing dark outside. I'd lost all sense of time.

I heard footsteps approaching my room. The handle wiggled, and there was a soft click. The door creaked open; I didn't dare open my eyes. The intruder's careful footsteps grow ever closer to the bed.

'Hey, sweetie.'

It was Mum. Honestly, I was glad to hear her voice.

'Can I sit?' she asked.

I unclenched my eyes and sat upright.

Mum perched herself beside me. I knew what she'd say next. It was a 'classic Mum line'.

'You can tell me anything,' she said.

But I couldn't. It was almost impossible to push the words out of my mouth. Phobos made sure of it. They somehow had control over my ability to speak. So, I said nothing.

'Well, you can tell me when you're ready. We're here for you. Remember that.'

I tried raising her a smile, but it felt fake and strained. Sometimes it takes a lot of effort to be happy. She got up off the bed and headed out of the room. Just before she left, I said, 'Mum ...'

She turned around and her face lit up. 'Yes, dear?'

'Do you believe in monsters?'

She scoffed at the mere thought. 'Why would you ask that?'

'No reason,' I said.

I could almost see the gears and cogs whirring in her head, trying to figure me out. 'So, you think it's monsters that did this to you?'

'No, that would be silly.' I laughed.

She offered me a plate of leftovers and left me alone with my thoughts.

The barn!

I slapped my forehead. *Idiot!* I rushed over to the window and peeked out of the gap in the blinds. It was difficult to see anything from there.

I hopped down off the bed and over to the telescope set up by the window, still fixed in the same position. I blew dust off the lens and peered down it.

It was dusk, but I could still see the hazy outline of the barn. The doors were wide open. The tarp sheet was still covering the unknown object inside. I could just make out a figure walking out. *It must be the farmer.* He had a torch and was in a hurry. A tractor was pulled up outside, with a trailer attached to the back. He was unspooling a long piece of rope.

Without warning, he pointed his torch right into my window. A blinding beam of light shone directly down the barrel of the telescope. I stayed glued to the spot. I was a deer frozen in headlights. My heart thumped against my chest. Maybe if I stayed still, he would simply ignore me, like a T-Rex. The light swept away again. The farmer carried on inside the barn. He heaved the barn doors shut; the sound of heavy wood clunked together in the distance. Again, the cries of an animal rang out into the empty night, its howls were almost recognisable, yet sounded like something not-of-this-earth. I had a suspicion we didn't have long before he moved the object. Maybe he saw me watching him. *We have to get in.*

7

THE PLAN

The following morning, Dad drove James, my younger brother, and me to school. I twiddled my thumbs nervously in the car. I felt so heavy. James sat quietly in the back, bleary-eyed, watching the world whizz by. He was in Year 2, still a baby in my parents' eyes. He never seemed interested in anything or talked very much. I always thought he got that from me. Dad shifted in his chair uncomfortably. He rolled down the window. The cool breeze wafted in and sent a shiver down my spine. It didn't help, adding to my state of fear.

I knew that after school that day, we would be doing a mission, for real, not just playing on the school field. This was outside in the real world, and, boy, did that scare me to death.

'So ...' Dad spoke up, which was even scarier because usually our morning drives were carried out in silence.

'Your mum told me you might have been a little bit upset yesterday.'

I continued staring forward at the road, unmoved by his attempts to communicate with me. 'Well, you know ... you can'—he stuttered profusely—'you can talk to me. I know your mum is good at that, and I ... I can help, too.'

I was taken aback. I wasn't used to Dad being so emotional.

I always related that with the typical 'stiff-upper-lip' way of thinking. We learned it at school. That phrase, meaning 'keep your cool', or 'don't show your weakness', originated far back as ancient Greece. Even if your leg was chopped off, if you cried, you weren't a real man.

I looked at Dad, if only briefly, and sat for a while longer. 'Thanks,' I murmured.

He smiled reassuringly. As I looked in the rear-view mirror, I saw James hadn't paid attention to a single word.

∽

THE BELL TRILLED. The whole class sat in a circle, gathered around our English teacher, Ms Trigger. She was much younger than most other teachers in the school, and she had a soothing, calm air about her.

She had emerald-green eyes and bleached blonde hair, standing out amongst the frumpy, lifeless teachers, who probably looked that way because they had been teaching for thirty years. I felt the most relaxed in her class, where I could be myself. It helped that I loved reading, and she'd often read stories that made us burst out laughing.

I sat with Bree and Tony, and I listened intently as the story circle began.

'Psst,' Bree whispered out the corner of her mouth.

I ignored her and instead focused on Ms Trigger. We were getting to the juicy part of the story.

'A hundred bloodthirsty badgers, armed with rifles, are going to attack Toad Hall this very night ...' she read.

'Haha!' I burst out laughing. I didn't mean to.

A few students shot me strange looks. I must have looked crazy.

'You strange, strange boy,' Phobos said. I could taste the shame and disappointment in his voice.

Ms Trigger giggled. 'That wasn't meant to be funny, but I'm glad you're paying attention.'

'Pssssst!'

That sounded more like a shout. I gave in. 'What?' I whispered through closed lips.

'Tell me the truth. What happened yesterday?' Bree asked.

Tony nudged me in the stomach. 'Ow ... Nothing.'

She leant over, locking me and Tony in her steely gaze.

'Look, if you don't want to tell me, then I'll go by myself tonight.'

She would literally torture us if it meant getting the truth.

'No, you won't!' Tony said. He called her bluff. 'You want to see what's in that barn just as much as we—'

'OK, Tony?'

Ms Trigger calmly caught him in her sights. 'Where did Mr Badger go?'

'Uh, to the willows?' he answered cluelessly. It was a well-educated guess, to be fair.

'No, but well done for remembering the title of the book,' she replied wittily.

Tony lowered his head. I felt his pain, too.

'Why does she always pick on me?' he muttered under his breath.

Unfortunately, Ms Trigger heard him. She snapped the book shut and peered directly into Tony's soul. I had never seen her mad, ever.

'I know the answer, Ms!' Bree said with her hand shooting eagerly in the air.

Ms Trigger sighed. 'OK, Bree. Go ahead.'

'To Toad Hall, Ms.'

'Correct.'

Bree looked smug with herself.

I tore off a piece of paper and scribbled down a note. I passed it behind Tony's back to Bree. It read: *Thomas and Dave tripped us.*

Her expression switched from frustration to empathy. She looked up at me and half-smiled. We had a silent understanding.

Bree beckoned us towards her. 'I have a plan. I'll tell you later,' she whispered.

8

PE

PE is a subject designed for the most popular, athletic kids in school. The coolest kids weren't into space, dinosaurs, or train models—they played sports.

I figured running track would be a great way to practise running away from bullies, at least. But when it came to football, I truly had two left feet. I couldn't process how they had such precise control of their lower body, as though it was as natural as writing with your toes. Maybe that's why I don't have much interest in the game, and maybe if I was better at it my life would be totally differ—

'Hey, snap out of it!' My daydream was rudely interrupted by Bree.

I shifted nervously on my feet. 'Hey, guys.'

'Hey, yourself.' Tony arrived kitted out in full footballer's attire. 'Just pretend you're defending and look busy,' he instructed like a secret agent.

I looked around, perplexed. 'Um, nobody's watching us.'

Tony slapped his head. 'Yeah, they wouldn't be very good spies if we knew they were listening to us.'

I shrugged in agreement.

The ground rumbled, and the earth shook. I gazed up to see the ball, followed by several opposing players, thundering down to our end of the pitch. My worst nightmare: participation. Without a word said, Tony took the lead and ran up to the player in possession of the ball. He slid across the ground like a knife through butter, knocking the boy over with ease. The ball went directly to our left-back player, who then took it to the other end.

Tony jogged back, brushing the dirt and bits of grass off his England shirt. He barely broke a sweat.

'So, Bree, what's this plan?' I asked.

She took a deep breath. 'So I have this secret informant, and his dad has this shop—'

'What kind of shop?' Tony interrupted.

'I'll tell you if you let me finish … I think it's a place where you can get stuff for your car, like spare parts and things. Anyway, they have all these tools like wrenches, jacks, pliers, and wire-cutters.'

Tony snapped his fingers. 'Perfect. You ask this "informant", whatever that means, and he gives us the tools. I'll bring the torch. Sorted.'

'Well …' She hesitated. 'What if his dad asks what we're using them for? Do we look like car mechanics?'

She made a great point. What would a bunch of ten-year-olds need with car repair tools? I felt that itch again; the grass irritated and poked at my ankles. The doubt started setting in.

'You could say they're for my dad!' Tony suggested.

Silence.

The bright, sunny day suddenly grew darker; looming clouds covered the sky, and a grey gloom fell. The sound of Bree's and Tony's bickering became muffled and distant.

'Hello, Will.' Phobos sneered. 'Tsk, tsk. What will your parents think? Breaking into private property? They'll disown you. They'll put you up for adoption in no time.'

I clasped my hands over my ears.

Phobos laughed. 'You think that'll help?'

I closed my eyes and breathed heavily. My heartbeat quickened.

'This is not going to work. You will get caught.'

A warm hand gently grabbed my wrist. My breathing slowed, and my heartbeat decreased. The sound of the birds chirping and stampeding children returned. I opened my eyes to see Bree's concerned face. 'Are you there?'

I looked at Tony. He'd seen me like this before.

'I'm here,' I said.

I felt safe again.

'Tackle him!'

The ground shook beneath our feet. We turned and squinted in the sunlight to find the source of the earthquake. As the light adjusted, we saw the football boys running in a perfect line at us, the ball hurtling straight towards me.

'You're defenders! Defend!' shouted our teammate.

I panicked and ran up to the ball. I kicked my leg pathetically into the air and missed entirely. I lost my balance and fell to the ground.

Their top striker passed me by and struck the ball with tremendous force into the back of the net. His team cheered and high-fived each other.

The striker approached us with his gang. His name was Nick. He was an athletic, typically handsome boy. He had bright blond hair, hazel eyes, and a mischievous smile. He always had his hands placed on his hips like he confidently owned any room he walked into.

'Hey, it's the weirdo gang. What you guys talking about?'

I recognized some of the other boys as I used to hang around with them. There was Benny, a humongous guy with an even bigger brain. I liked him. He was kind when the football boys weren't around. There was also Alex, an even bigger guy, with a smaller brain. We called him 'Mount Everest' because he cast a shadow over the entire playground.

The boys grinned as they were about to partake in some good old-fashioned verbal torture.

Tony was the first to speak up. 'Hey, nice goal, Nick. But we're having this meeting. It's kind of private, so ...'

Nick ignored him entirely. He kept his attention on Bree. 'I heard people talk about you. You call this thing The Mystery, right?'

The boys laughed heartily as though they were reading signs that said CHEER NOW.

Bree kept on smiling at them. It didn't bother her in the slightest. I, on the other hand, was sweating buckets.

'That's pretty sad, you know? You actually believe in aliens and stuff?'

Tony looked as if he wanted to smack Nick. I shook my head at him. *Leave it,* I communicated telepathically.

Nick was deadlocked on Bree. It was as if I didn't exist.

'I'm not surprised at you, weird girl, but you'—he turned his attention to Tony—'you would make a good player. Why don't you come play with us?'

Tony looked down, ashamed. I think he might have even considered the idea. Bree got up and calmly walked over to him, almost touching his face. Nick backed up a little. She smiled and said, 'I don't think he wants to join you. In fact, I think we're all just fine here. Why don't you go chase a ball around a field.'

I couldn't help but smile, too.

Nick stepped forward again, now towering over Bree. He met her gaze and didn't break eye contact for what felt like an hour. 'You. I saw you go into the woods.'

I perked my head up. He was talking to me but kept his eyes firmly on her. 'Yeah, you ran out of there like you saw a ghost,' he said.

Tony turned to me, surprised.

'N-no, I was just looking ...' I stuttered.

'Well? What did you see?' his voice grew louder.

'N-nothing, I ...'

Mr Owens, the PE teacher, blew his whistle at us. 'Break it up!' he yelled.

'OK, you don't want to tell me. Fine. Enjoy your weird friends.' Nick smirked and turned away, beckoning his gang to join.

We stood mostly in silence for the rest of the uneventful game, but Tony and I were quietly admiring Bree.

'Tonight. School gates. Four p.m.,' Bree said.

9

THE NEWSAGENT DEBACLE

I kept looking at my watch over and over again. It was already way past four p.m., and Tony was nowhere to be seen.

Me and Bree had been hanging around outside the school building for around twenty minutes. The anticipation and nerves started to kick in. If we were too late, the farmer could have already moved that thing in the barn by now. And then who would believe me?

Tony finally came out to join us, his face full of excitement. 'Hey, guys. Let's go.'

'About time!' Bree said.

'W ... Wa ... Wait,' I stuttered as we came to a standstill just in front of the gate at the entrance of the school.

Bree tapped her foot impatiently. 'What's the matter?'

I took a moment to observe the spiky prison-like gate. 'It's ... We've never done The Mystery outside before.'

She wasn't mad. Instead, she grinned. "Take the adventure, heed the call, now ere the irrevocable moment passes!"

'Huh?'

Bree grimaced. 'Don't you pay attention to anything in class?'

'Come on!' Tony said.

I took my first step past the dreaded barrier of iron. The rest that followed were surprisingly easy after that.

We started sprinting down the road—our destination: Alan's Car Parts.

~

THE TOWN HALL had a ginormous clock tower that loomed over the entire town. It was the landmark of Barnsmead. All the boutique shops, butchers, and markets all lived under its shadow.

The main road paved through the town centre was short enough you could walk the entire distance in under ten minutes. I would know because on my weekend shopping visits with my family, I'd speed-run the entire thing. I hated being in the presence of so many people at once. There's something about people all gathering in one place that creeps me out. Why does everyone feel the need to be always so close together?

We made it to the tower; it read 4:30 p.m. The giant clock gonged loudly.

The sun was setting over the rows of chimneys all lined down the street, and the orange glow acted like a beacon, guiding our way there.

Look natural, I thought. *Nobody knows what we're doing.*

'Are you sure about that?' Phobos asked.

We pushed through a crowd of people with our heads down. I was wary of studious eyes surrounding us. I could have sworn their owners were purposely getting in our way. The sunset began to emit a more ominous reddish colour; it backlit the strangers' heads, casting them into shadowy figures.

I tried to keep up with Bree and Tony, who were now gaining further ahead as they slipped through the narrowing gaps in the crowd. I lost them. It wasn't long before I realized I was fully encircled. The tall, dark silhouettes stood perfectly still; their faces had no clear features, eyes, nose, mouth, anything. Again, those familiar whispers began to rise from the depths of quietness. *'Where's he going?'*

'Where are his parents?'

I whipped around only to confront more faceless figures.

'He's a little thug.'

The circle started closing in, tightening their grip further. I was almost in their clutches.

'He's going to get caught. I can't believe he threw away his education for this.'

The only way forward was to go down, so I slumped onto the floor and curled up into a ball.

'Is that Will?' said another voice.

Huh? That sounded like Nick, I thought.

I looked up. 'Oh.'

Nick stood over me, shoulder to shoulder with Thomas, Dave, and Alex. They all peered down, looking bemused at my sad state, curled up on the floor.

'He's so weird.' Thomas laughed, obnoxiously chewing his gum.

'Nah, he's just being funny,' Nick snorted. 'Aren't you, mate?'

I wasn't, but it was a good cover. 'Yeah, I was just messing around. You got me.'

I laughed it off as Nick pulled me up with one arm. There was an awkward pause as I stood around waiting for the conversation to continue.

Nick slapped his hands together. 'So, we're going to hit the newsagents.'

The boys all nodded; they had a troublesome look in their eyes.

'OK, that's cool. I think I need to—'

'Come with us,' Nick suggested generously.

'Oh, well ...' I looked at their faces. They didn't care if I went or not, but an invite from Nick, the coolest kid in school (and thereby my world) wasn't something to turn down.

'I bet he doesn't even get pocket money,' Dave said under his breath.

I gritted my teeth. 'I guess I could get some sweets.'

～

AT THE NEWSAGENTS, the aisles were lined with pick 'n' mix, magazines, toys—a one-stop destination for any kid. The boys slunk around, picking up copies of the *Beano* and reading most of it before putting it back. I pretended to browse the pick 'n' mix, knowing full well my pockets were empty. This was a massive waste of time. I needed to get back to The Mystery gang.

Where are Bree and Tony? Did they make it to the shop without me? Do we still have time? As these thoughts raced around my mind, I didn't notice Nick sneak up behind me.

He tapped me on the back. 'Hey. Open your hand.'

I glanced down to see Nick with a handful of sweets. *Is he hinting I do something?*

He smacked the sweets into my hand, and I snapped it shut like a crocodile snatching its prey. *Am I really about to do this?* I took a glance at the shopkeeper. He was busy with a customer, carefully counting the coins he was handed.

I moved my closed fist down to my pocket and released the contents inside. Nick patted me on the shoulder as if I was some sort of hero. I wasn't.

I don't know if the shopkeeper was watching us as we waltzed on past him. I didn't dare look back. An intense cloud of guilt welled up inside.

Outside the shop, the gang joined and slapped me on the back, one by one.

'You're crazy, mate!'

'I can't believe you actually did it.'

I turned to Nick, who was standing there like nothing had happened. I instinctively pulled the sweets from my pocket and handed them over.

'Oh, you took these?' Nick accused.

'I thought you—'

'You thought I what?'

I was taken aback, and he grinned like he'd pulled off a great trick.

'Nothing,' I said, letting out a sigh of defeat.

He snatched the sweets out of my hand, then stuffed his face with the stolen goods.

I have to tell the shopkeeper, I thought. I turned to go inside the shop, but Phobos pulled me back.

'Are you stupid? He's going to call the police. Just shut up and find them,' they snapped.

'There you are!' someone yelled behind me.

I swung around to see Tony sprinting right at us. 'Where'd you go?' he asked. 'We looked everywhere for you.'

'Tony!' Nick yelled. He seemed full of excitement for some reason.

'Oh, hi, Nick ... what are you guys doing?'

Just out of view of the football boys, I mimed zipping my lips shut. I wanted to leave the situation ASAP.

'We're gonna play a game down at Priory Lane. You should come,' Nick said.

'Uh. Well. I'm kinda busy so—'

'Let's just go. He wants to stay with his boring mate,' Alex said, rolling his eyes and checking his watch.

'I know you've got skills. I reckon you could join the team,' Nick said.

'Really?' Thomas said, unable to believe what he was hearing.

'Yes.'

I noticed that same pained look on Tony's face. The look that said he didn't want to leave us behind, but he didn't have a choice. I couldn't force him to stay, but at the same time I needed him.

'OK, I'll go.' Tony said. As he passed me by, he whispered in my ear, 'Help me. Say something ...'

But I didn't help him. I stood there like a useless lemon and said nothing at all.

Nick slung his arm over Tony like they'd been best friends for years, and the boys took off. But not all of them. Two stayed behind.

I felt the heavy thud of a sweaty hand land on my shoulder.

'Not you,' Thomas said.

I shifted my weight from one foot to another. I had to find Bree. We were losing light and time. I looked up at the clock tower, which now read 5:00 p.m.

'Whatever this thing is, we wanna see it,' Thomas said.

'Yeah!' Dave said.

'S-see what?'

'That thing—whatever's in that barn.'

I couldn't believe I'd been so stupid. They must have

overheard everything. The mission was officially compromised.

'Well ... I—' I couldn't force the words out.

'We could always tell the shopkeeper what we just saw, couldn't we, Dave?'

'We could.' Dave replied.

I was a leaf caught in a storm. I really had no choice now.

'Don't mind if we join you then?' Thomas cackled.

Before I could reply, the two boys grabbed me forcefully by the shoulders.

'Nah, thought not.' And off we went.

∼

AFTER ALMOST HALF A MILE, I finally spotted the glowing yellow neon sign: ALAN'S CAR PARTS.

I stopped just short of the entrance. I had a moment to reflect on what had just happened. The offences were stacking up by the minute. *Am I a criminal?* I asked myself.

'Yes. Yes, you are!' barked Phobos.

Bree appeared from the doorway and turned to me, grinning.

'Hey! Oh ...' She looked the two boys up and down. They gave her a wave with huge grins on their faces.

She pulled me to one side and whispered, 'What happened back there? Where's Tony?'

I looked over my shoulder at the boys, then back at Bree. I shrugged. 'Just bumped into some ... friends. Just go along with it. Anyway, did you get the thing?'

Before she could answer, a big, lumbering figure exited the shop. He pulled down his hoodie.

'Oh, hi, Benny, what are you doing here?' It took my stupid brain a minute to process.

Bree had to spell out the obvious for me. 'Will, he's the informant.'

'Benjamin! You helping these freaks?' Thomas asked.

Benny looked like a mouse caught in a trap. He quickly pulled out a pair of small shiny scissors and handed them over to Bree.

'That's the wire-cutter?' I asked.

'Do you think my dad would give me wire-cutters? This is the best I could do,' he said.

I slapped my forehead hard.

Bree rolled her eyes. 'You're so whiney. This is the next best thing.'

She handed Benny the money for our 'wire-cutters'. I pinched my nose in frustration. Phobos rubbed it in a little deeper. *You risked everything ... for this?*

I calmed myself down. 'OK, it'll have to do.'

Benny flicked up his hood and skulked off back inside.

'Let's go, weirdos.' Thomas and Dave slapped their hands on both our backs and steered us away.

10

THE BREAK-IN

It was dusk and the sun had officially set over the Dower hills. A deep blue sky barely illuminated the field ahead of us. We stood at the edge, in front of the long metal fence that surrounded it. I was quivering uncontrollably. I could barely move. There was a calm and quiet atmosphere I wasn't expecting. I became highly aware of my surroundings and the gravity of what we were about to do.

Bree pulled the scissors out of the bag and reached towards the fence. She extended the jaws, getting dangerously close to the first wire. Something wasn't right. I noticed the cows grazing in the field.

'Do you hear that buzzing sound?' Dave asked Thomas.

I made a dash straight towards the scissors and batted them right out of her hand. She wrenched herself up.

'What are you doing?' she scolded.

I pointed at a small triangular sign nestled in a bush, a bolt of lightning with the word WARNING engraved into it. Her breath shuddered.

'I can't believe I almost did that. I would have been electrocuted ...'

'You're welcome,' said Dave.

I couldn't help but laugh out of nervousness. 'It's OK. You know, we could just go home. Maybe this was a sign. Your mum and dad must be worried.'

She paused briefly, like I'd struck a nerve. Perhaps we had gone too far.

I turned to see Thomas and Dave, who folded their arms and shook their heads. There was no going back.

Bree studied the fence and noted the tree leaning against it. 'Can you climb?' she asked.

'You better!' said Thomas.

'No, you bloody can't,' Phobos helpfully answered.

Have you ever tried to climb a tree? It's difficult. Like, ridiculously difficult. If you've got no support, you're just clinging onto a vertical surface with nothing but useless human hands to hold on. There's a reason we don't live in trees. I had these unhelpful thoughts as I hung onto a branch halfway up. I could already feel splinters digging into my palms.

'Now swing!' Bree shouted at me, pumping her arms in the air.

'I'm not a monkey!' I yelled back at her.

Thomas and Dave were doubling over in fits of laughter. If they weren't so interested in the barn, I suspected they would have loved me to fall and break my legs.

I could see the barn closer than ever before. I found some extra fuel in the tank and mustered all my strength. I began to swing back and forth, gathering momentum.

'Oh, you're so *not going to make it,'* Phobos taunted. *'You're just not the athletic type.'*

Shut up! I snapped back.

The fence passed clearly below me, but I waited until

the last possible second. I swung the farthest yet and took my chance. *Now!*

I leapt and cleared the fence by miles, landing terribly in the mud below with a big *SPLAT!*

'Wooo! Will, king of the monkeys,' Bree cried as she celebrated in the background.

'I'm not a monkey. I'm a polar bear,' I muttered under my breath.

'What?'

Oh no, she heard me. 'Nothing!'

It wasn't long until Bree cleared the fence and joined me at my side. Thomas and Dave followed closely after. We cautiously walked onwards through the long grass, the sounds of chirping crickets and mooing cows accompanying us. There was an eerie rumbling of the ground as we neared the barn.

The lights were off, not a person in sight. We got so close to the giant double doors we could practically touch them. The sky was now pitch black, and the only source of light was the light pollution radiating from the town behind the Dower hills. We exchanged looks of concern, but Bree had a glint of adventure in her eyes and wasn't going to quit now. I, on the other hand, probably looked as if I wanted to eat myself and disappear from existence.

'For The Mystery,' Bree said, clenching her fist into a ball.

'The Mystery,' I replied, my hands trembling.

~

BREE WAS the first to reach the barn. She placed her hand on the worn wooden door. She remained completely still, like she was paused. I stayed further back, scared she had seen something.

'Bree,' I whispered. 'Why'd you stop?'

She kept facing forwards, hand firmly pressed against the door. 'What if this changes everything? What if ... What if it's real?'

The weight of each word hit me like a freight train. I never anticipated our investigations to amount to something real. I mustered up the courage to speak. 'Open it.'

The doors creaked loudly. They thudded against the walls. Inside lay total piercing darkness. We took our first steps inside, lifting our legs up and over the lip of the barn door. The cold stone floor echoed our steps around the vast space. I held onto her arm, but she didn't seem to notice.

'I can't see, where's the torch?' Bree asked.

'Tony had it, remember?'

We took a few more steps inside. The rustling of grass alarmed me. I spun around to find the source. It came from the field somewhere nearby.

'The farmer's coming. He's going to find you,' Phobos said.

I figured they might be right.

'Hurry up.' I shook her arm.

She ignored my pleas and stayed focused. We took a few more steps, now reaching the centre of the room.

CLANG!

My head struck a metallic object, the sound of which rang out. We lurched back, squinted at the object, and as we adjusted to the darkness, our eyes lit up with equal measures of fear and wonder. There it was, just as I observed through my telescope. A round, spherical disc stood magnificently in the middle of the barn. It was covered with sheets, but we could already tell what it was.

Bree turned to me, her mouth agape and eyes wide as saucers. 'It's ... It's a—'

'It's an alien!' Thomas blurted out.

'Just a UFO ... actually,' I said softly.

Dave bonked my head. I adjusted my messed-up hair.

We only needed to do one last thing to prove our theory. I grabbed one end of the sheet, and Bree grabbed the other end.

'No, I wanna do it!' Thomas demanded. He pushed us out of the way, and Dave joined him by his side.

We exchanged looks of worry.

'One, two, three ... pull!'

They tugged and pulled the material off in one massive heave. As the sheets fell away, we were met with striking silver machinery. Its surface was covered with vents and gadgets I couldn't describe. The body looked damaged—scratches and dents covered it. The presumed engine lay under the main body and the entire ship was floating off the ground. It hovered, bobbing up and down. The cockpit was in the middle, and the glass that housed the pilot was frosted, so it was impossible to see inside. We both stepped back in amazement. Was I dreaming? No, I couldn't be. My dreams were way more boring than this. It was real.

Bree circled the UFO, taking in all the detail she could.

'I did tell you ...' I said proudly. It was nice to be proven right for a change.

'Inside. Do you think there's a ... an—'

'Alien?' She nodded. 'If there's a ship, there's a pilot. I need to take notes.' Bree took out a notepad and scribbled frantically.

A beam of light shone through the window. It was coming from outside. We turned sharply to see a figure coming at us. 'It's the farmer!' Dave shrieked.

I could hear barking. *Great, and he brought dogs, too!*

I'm sure we looked utterly helpless, flailing our arms and running aimlessly as the light grew closer.

'Where do we go?' I yelled at Bree in pure panic.

'We can't get out. The tree's on the other side of the fence.'

She was right. Why does she always have to be right?

'We've got this. We can take him,' Thomas said, taking a fighting stance.

'No,' I said.

Everyone turned and faced me, expecting some grand plan. I took the lead and ran towards the barn doors. 'Here, I'll close this, you close the other one.'

Bree looked as though I was mad. 'With us still inside?'

'You want to go outside?'

She looked defeated. We were out of ideas and time. We forced the doors closed with an almighty slam. If the farmer didn't know we were here before, he did now.

'Under here.' I propped up the sheets, and we all crawled underneath.

Just as our legs slithered under, the doors burst open. The dogs barked aggressively and began hunting for signs of life. They were first drawn to the UFO, sniffing around it. *'You're so dead!'* Phobos laughed devilishly.

The dogs turned their attention to our hiding spot. I could hear their growls drawing closer. I felt something in my trousers as I shifted. There was still a sweet in my pocket! I wiggled it out and thrust it out the front door. The dogs chased after it. Shortly after, the farmer came bounding inside, his blinding torchlight scanning the room. He mechanically paced around the room like a T-1000 robot.

'I saw you boys come in here.' His gravelly voice

boomed. 'You look like kids, so I'm gonna go easy on ya.' He shifted his gaze across the room and landed squarely on the sheets messily draped across the floor. He'd found us.

'What you saw in here was my little experiment, nothing more. I made it. Whatever you *think* you saw is just little kiddys' imagination gone wild.'

His feet were now placed firmly in front of me, with only a thin layer of material separating us. The distraction I created was only temporary. The dogs were back, and they knew exactly where we were. They began gnawing and tugging at the sheet with their teeth.

'Got any more sweets?' Dave pleaded.

I hadn't.

'Will? What are we going to do? Will?' Bree was panicking, and I wasn't any use.

The coarse material that helped hide us was now wrapping around my neck. It constricted my airway like a python. I gasped for air, grasping and pulling the sheet, but it only got tighter.

'Do something, idiots!' Thomas shouted.

'This is where it ends.' Phobos's voice slithered and hissed through the air. *'You're no use to anyone. Your feeble arms, your cowardly brain ...'*

I gave in. They were right. I was no hero. So, I just lay there, waiting for the farmer to find us.

The harsh glow of the light was now directly in our eyes. We recoiled from being blinded. But this wasn't the farmer's torch. It wasn't a white light. It was green. A bellowing horn blared out. The dogs scampered away. The sheets peeled away from us and flew out the door.

I opened my eyes. The UFO was lit up like a Christmas tree. Its vents were pouring out hot air and the wind kicked up dust all around us. Bree and I ran backwards over to the wall and pressed up against it. The farmer dropped his torch and gawped at the magnificent machine. The engines began spooling up and the noise grew louder as it gained power.

'Look what you've done!' said the farmer through tears. 'We're all done for.'

The UFO started forward, hovering directly over him. The bottom opened up like a flower unfurling, and a concentrated beam of pure green light encased him. The farmer began to float upwards into the machine. He floated up and up until he disappeared inside the UFO. The light vanished in a flash. Bree and I looked on, unable to speak a word.

'Leave 'em!' Thomas and Dave bolted for the exit. As they made their escape, in their fear-stricken state, they forgot to step over the lip of the barn door. They both tripped and tumbled over each other, striking the muddy floor with their big clumsy bodies.

The UFO darted over to them in an instant. The steely bottom unfurled. They were soon awash in the deadly green light. They looked upwards in utter fear and hugged each other tightly as they disappeared into its belly.

Then, another peculiar thing happened. The light returned, but it wasn't a pure tunnel of green. It flashed several times in different sequences. It was as though the machine was trying to speak. Bree, with a trembling hand, pulled out her notebook, trying to decipher whatever it was doing.

.-.. . .- ...- . / -- . / .- .-.. --- -. .

Before she could finish, the light extinguished for good.

With one enormous blast of energy, the ship burst through the roof, splintering the wooden beams into thousands of pieces.

The chaos was silenced in an instant. Shards of wood

rained down, but they landed gently around us like falling snow. I wanted to say something, but words would not be enough to express what we had just witnessed.

We headed back to the electric fence, which was now disabled. Somehow the UFO had killed all power in the area as it activated. At least, that was our theory.

We walked home that evening, covered in flakes of sawdust and dirt. We didn't say much. I think we were a little traumatized. At the town centre, we were ready to part ways. Before we did, Bree stared at me with a haunting look I'll never forget.

'Will ...' she said, in a hushed tone, 'it could have taken us, but it didn't. And I have no idea why.'

Bree knew everything, and she was always so sure of herself, but not this time. It scared the living daylights out of me. But it got me thinking. *Why didn't it take us?*

We reluctantly returned to our homes. I cannot describe this next part in detail, as it seems to blur into memories I crammed away in the hard-to-reach corners of my brain. I remember the shooting looks of disappointment from my mother and the baritone voice of my father shouting at me. The shopkeeper from the newsagents had called. It turned out he had cameras installed. He saw everything. I wasn't allowed back in there for at least a year.

I could only imagine Bree's family and their reaction. She came from a well-off family, you could say. They certainly had more money than the average family and had their reputation to uphold.

I think Tony dodged a bullet that day—the most stressful thing he had to do was play a game of football with Nick and the boys. Now that I say it out loud, that actually sounds worse.

11

CONKERS

The day after our otherworldly encounter, the leaves had darkened and wilted. The air turned bitter and harsh. The year was passing by at a record pace. It's true what they say: time goes faster as you get older.

Every year there was a new trend. Last year it was football cards, the year before that was friendship bracelets. But at this time of year, everything else was dropped for one special seasonal contest. It was late autumn, which meant conker season was upon us.

The entire school was out in the playground, smashing them together like wrecking balls. The first lucky students there always got the pick of the largest.

The conkers, otherwise known as chestnuts, were plucked from their spiky shells, then threaded through with string and tied in a knot. Two players would take turns hitting their conkers against the other's. Whoever broke their opponent's conker first would be the winner. The champions were usually the bigger, stronger kids who wouldn't flinch as they collided and blew their rival to pieces.

Bree and I roamed the edges of the playground, watching everyone gather round and cheer on the players.

'Any more sightings?' Bree asked, her notebook at the ready.

I kicked the gravel carelessly. 'No. Nothing.'

Bree was pacing up and down. I'd never seen her so worried. 'Where do you think it went? What happened to ... you know?' she asked.

I didn't care much about what happened to Thomas and Dave, to be honest. I was almost glad they were gone.

'I'm sure they're fine ... they probably just got dropped off somewhere,' I said. But I wasn't really paying attention.

I was focused on Tony and Charlene, who were playing their own game of conkers, away from the hysterical hyenas at the centre of the playground. Over the past few days or so, I noticed he seemed to have grown much closer with her. Some new uncomfortable feeling began to develop. It rumbled and roared in my belly like a growing fire.

Phobos picked their moment. *'Should have spoken to her sooner. Wimp.'*

I will speak to her, there's still time.

'Oh really? Because I think your time was up long ago.'

The school bell rang, and everyone headed inside. As the playground emptied, I went over to Tony with my hands placed firmly in my trouser pockets.

'Hey,' I shouted over to him.

He and Charlene were packing up their game, ready to leave.

'Hi, um ...' Charlene smiled politely.

'Will,' Tony said.

'That's it! Will.'

I led Tony by the hand and took him to one side. 'Hey, can we talk?'

'OK. What did you wanna talk about?' he asked.

Something was up. His voice was monotone, and his eyes didn't sparkle like they usually did. He almost looked zombified.

'You should have seen it; it was amazing,' I said.

'I'm sure it was,' Tony replied.

'Well ... you must have had fun with the football boys.'

'Actually ... it was pretty fun.'

'Oh. Cool,' I said through gritted teeth.

'Yeah. And Nick introduced me to Charlene. I can't believe it. She talks to me all the time now!'

That new feeling rolled around uncomfortably in my belly.

'Huh. I guess Tony really made a good impression with the football boys. They must really like him,' Phobos said.

So? I don't care,

Their excitement was palpable. Phobos enjoyed every second of my misery.

'He must be growing tired of all this baby stuff.'

Shut up. PLEASE. Shut up.

'He's growing up. Unlike you. You're growing down!'

'They don't like you!' I blurted out.

Tony leapt back. I imagined how insane I must have looked.

'Well ... you could have said something. You just let me go with them,' he said.

He had me there. It was true. But when the most popular boy in school asks you to play football, you don't say no.

'Tony, we're going to be late for class,' Charlene urged.

He nodded, and they left me in the cold, drizzly playground. The wind picked up and whipped my face. Perhaps Phobos was onto something. We were in Year 6. Secondary school was just around the corner. We *were* growing up. I guessed Tony was more interested in girls. Girls that I had no chance with.

Unless ...

~

I SKIPPED LUNCH THAT DAY. As soon as the clock struck twelve, I zoomed out the door and straight into the playing field. Chestnut trees were dotted around the edges. I sifted through the shrivelled mouldy conkers to find a decent one.

I looked down at my chosen conker. It was meek, wimpy, and looked like it might explode with a small squeeze. I had to play. If there was a chance it might impress Charlene, I had to take it.

I stepped out into the playground and was immediately hit with the screams and cheers of students. My whole body felt tingly and strange. It brought me back to my encounter with the beast in the woods, but somehow this felt scarier. The stakes were high as players were eliminated left and right. I was drawn to the centre of the playground, where there seemed to be a lot of excitement. I poked my head through the crowd; two boys were playing a match. I recognised the bigger boy instantly. It was Alex, one of the football boys. Beside them were four students with dangling bits of string and mangled shells hanging from them. They were sobbing. Alex looked like he was winding up for one last swing.

'Smash it!' the crowd yelled.

He lifted his arm, flicked back the conker, and brought it down on his opponent's. With pinpoint accuracy, he struck with such force the nut came apart completely, shattering into tiny pieces. The student whimpered and forced his way through the crowd, humiliated. Everyone clapped at this impressive display, as if they saw a gladiator bring down a tiger.

Alex threw his hands in the air and scanned the crowd, looking for his next victim.

'Come on! Five down. Who's next?'

Everyone shuffled backwards, afraid to be added to the pile of bodies. I ducked down, hoping I wouldn't be recognised.

'Hey, weirdo, that you?' the thuggish voice called out.

'Ooo, he saw you,' Phobos teased. *'You better go. These students will eat you alive if you don't.'*

I timidly stuck my hand in the air. Alex beckoned me over. The crowd made an entrance for me. This could be the match of the century, but somehow, I doubted it. I came face-to-face with the big brute. He smiled half-cocked.

'Let's go. It'll be quick, I promise.'

He may have been a little dim, but he wasn't wrong. I pulled back my conker, copying what I saw before.

'Um, he goes first,' said an unknown voice from the crowd.

'Yeah, the winner goes first,' said another.

I lowered my hand, then gulped. How embarrassing. I could hear the whispers rising. The chattering got louder, but I refused to let them form into words I could hear. I scanned the crowd, hoping to see a glimpse of Charlene, but all I saw was a smear of faceless people.

Alex raised his conker, winding the string tightly around his fingers. Without warning, he came down hard on top of mine. I jerked back my head and screwed my eyes shut.

THWACK!

The vibration ran down my arm—a sharp, painful sting. He had hit my thumb. I sucked in the pain and kissed my teeth. Nobody could know it hurt. Nobody. I opened my eyes and looked down. To my amazement, my conker was still intact; only the surface was peeled away. I laughed nervously. Alex looked annoyed. He always won on the first hit, but I suppose my stupid thumb got in the way.

It was my turn. I raised my conker up again. The voices grew louder.

'Miss. Miss. Miss.'

Phobos joined in, too. *'Miss! Miss! Miss!'*

With all my strength I whipped it back and swung downwards as hard as I possibly could. A stillness fell over the crowd. I looked down. I'd missed. I'd missed by a wide mile. The laughter that rose was so loud it attracted others to come over and see what was so funny. My cheeks were burning like a human furnace. They must have looked redder than a fire engine. It was over. My social life. My reputation. My chance to impress Charlene. I wasn't good for anything. I held out my string, despairing. I glanced at Alex for only a second, but even he seemed to look a little embarrassed for me. Immediately he cracked my conker in two halves. He gave me the courtesy of a swift defeat.

He walked over to me, and I cowered, expecting a wedgie or maybe a rope burn. Instead, he bent down and whispered in my ear. 'Listen careful, like. Not many kids get this ...'

I nodded and listened intently to every word.

He continued. 'The winter dance is one month next. If you play me again and win, I'll get you dancing with Charlene.'

I backed away, waving my hands. 'No, I ... I don't—'

He pulled me back with his gigantic hand, so close his

slimy breath washed over me. 'It's cool, I know you like her. Rematch. Tuesday lunchtime. Let's shake on it.'

He stretched out his hand, awaiting mine. I was apprehensive. I thought it was too good to be true. What was the catch? There's always a catch. But when would I get an opportunity like this again?

'OK, t-thank you.' We shook hands, and the deal was made.

12

GRANDPARENTS VISIT

On the weekend of my miserable loss, I stayed the entire time indoors. My grandparents were visiting; they had travelled down from Yorkshire. My grandma loved spending time with us, talking about everything, from politics to silly stories. She didn't treat us like kids, more like mini adults. My grandad would sit on the sofa the entire time. I don't recall seeing him move, ever. He was a grouchy grandad. The kind that would moan about the rain even though they didn't go outside. Nothing impressed him.

We were all sitting in the living room, gathered around the TV. I tuned out the conversation, as I always did when adults were talking. My brother and I stared at the big square box. I rubbed my thumb. It had turned purple from the blood built up underneath the nail.

I bet Alex could have taken off my whole finger if he wanted to, I thought.

I turned to my brother, who was still transfixed on the TV. 'Pssst. James.'

He didn't budge. He was watching *Power Ninjas*; there

was no way to break his concentration. My attempts at communication were caught by Grandma. 'So then, stranger ...'

I raised my head like a meerkat.

'What have you been up to, eh? What's school like these days?'

Mum and Dad looked alarmed.

'Not much,' I said. It was sort of the truth. 'I ... I joined the chess club.'

She looked impressed. She put on her glasses to get a better look at me. 'Chess, eh? That's a game for geniuses. You know that billionaire? Phil ... what's his name?'

'Baxton,' Dad said.

'Yes, that's it. He plays chess, and *he* did well at school.'

'Didn't he drop out of school?' Mum added.

'Well, it did help he went to Harvard. Not exactly public school,' Dad said.

Grandad awakened out of the blue to change the TV channel to the evening news. James just stared at him, seething with rage.

Their conversation moved away from me to other things. I needed to leave the room.

I made my move to the gaming den whilst the adults were distracted. James saw this and followed me inside.

'Can we play Death-Squirrel?' he asked.

'No ... this is a top-secret meeting,' I said, gently closing the door behind me.

He perked up and shifted over to me. 'Is it about the ghost?'

'What? Oh no, that was fake. This is real.'

His eyes widened. James had a passion for seeking the supernatural and the unknown, too, but he was only six years old, so he couldn't handle the mature parts like I could.

I turned on the games console. The whirring disk and loud start-up jingle made the perfect distraction.

'You want to hear something top secret?'

He inched closer and nodded.

'Me and my friend found something. It was this flying machine. When we got close, it flew away.'

'Like a plane?' he asked.

'Kind of. More like a spaceship. But I don't think it came from here.'

'From Barnsmead?'

'No, like from Earth.'

His eyes widened even further.

'I think it wanted to help. It saved us.'

James looked puzzled. He scrunched his face up, and I noticed a scratch under his eye. 'What happened?' I asked, pointing to his injury.

His mood changed in an instant. He looked away so I couldn't see his face. I tried to approach the situation carefully, knowing he was upset. 'You know, I bet the UFO could help you too ...'

He looked up at me with puppy-dog eyes. 'Really?' He sniffed. As he faced me directly, I could now see his scratch clearly. It looked like a fingernail had clawed at him.

I nodded. 'I think it likes us. It could have got me and Bree, but it didn't.'

He seemed to relax.

'Just keep looking at the sky,' I said.

We both looked out the window. The sky was dark and brewing with grey clouds. We both wondered what could be out there.

～

THE NEXT DAY WAS SUNDAY, the worst day of the weekend. It served only as a reminder that tomorrow was Monday, and a full week of school—a.k.a. a living nightmare—awaited.

Me, James, and Grandma were taking a stroll through the local woods, fully kitted out in thick coats and woolly gloves.

She was a calming presence to be around, never intimidating like most adults. I knew she was about to ask me something, but the calming winds blowing through the trees helped sooth my nerves.

'Your mum told me about school.' She stopped in her tracks. 'You don't have to say anything.'

That was comforting. Sometimes I just wanted to sit and listen, no pressure to talk all the time.

She continued. 'You're like your dad, you know. And you, James.'

I groaned internally. James rolled his eyes.

'He was one of four boys. Four! Can you imagine having four young, crazy boys running around the house all day?' She laughed to herself. 'Your dad liked to play outside a lot. It made him strong and tough. He would swing on trees, play in the mud, come home such a mess. I would get so mad at him.'

I cracked a slight smile. That sounded familiar.

We came to a stop and rested on a nearby bench.

'One day he came home from school, and I could tell he was upset. He didn't say anything, I just knew. I left him alone. If I told his older brothers, they'd tease him all week. The next day the same thing happened. He came home and slammed his bedroom door. I went in this time and saw bruises on his arms.'

I drew closer to her. I had no idea Dad got bullied before. He'd never mentioned his childhood, not once.

She continued. 'I pulled him up gently and simply said, "Next time you see that bully, you punch him square in the mouth".'

I was slightly shaken by Grandma's bluntness. I clasped my hands over my mouth dramatically. James clapped in delight. He seemed to enjoy that.

'Your dad was the smallest in the family, but you can't judge a person by their size, right, boys?'

We nodded in agreement.

'The next day, that boy went over to your dad and knocked his lunchbox onto the floor. He smiled at him, which confused the boy, and then popped him right in the mouth.'

James was fully invested in the story by this point. I knew Grandma was cool, but she just went a dozen ranks higher on my list.

'Guess what happened after that? Nothing. That boy never laid a finger on him again.'

As we continued onwards, I thought carefully about Grandma's story, and just being around her made me feel a little tougher.

We soon stumbled across a litter of chestnuts spread across the leaf-strewn ground. She chuckled. 'I remember playing with these!'

I couldn't believe it.

'You played conkers, Grandma?'

'Of course I did. We've probably been playing with these for as long as there were trees around.' She bent down and examined the floor, rummaging through the shrivelled shells. 'Ah. Here we go.'

She picked up a medium-sized one. It didn't look like anything special, but she was sure this was the winner.

'Grandma. I don't think I'm ... strong enough to play,' I said.

'Nonsense. Come on, I've got a trick to show you.'

~

LATER THAT EVENING, Mum was preparing dinner in the kitchen. It was Sunday, and we had company, so obviously we were going to have an epic roast dinner fit for royalty. This usually consisted of mashed potatoes, stuffing, chicken, roast potatoes, vegetables, and thick brown gravy. As Mum worked her magic in the kitchen, Grandma was sifting through the cupboards. She barged Mum out of the way.

'What are you looking for?' Mum said, annoyed as she juggled pots, pans, and chopping knives. I swear she had a secret third hand.

'Never you mind!' said Grandma as she produced a large jug of vinegar from the top shelf. She poured the vinegar into a plastic tub and placed the conker inside. I pulled away in disgust; the smell was overwhelming.

'Now, leave it in here for at least three or four days,' she instructed. 'It will harden the conker, making it stronger. You're going to beat that boy by the end of the week.'

I certainly thought she was mad, but she had lived through it all, so it'd be foolish for me to doubt her now.

13

THE AMPHITHEATRE

It was Monday already. I avoided the playground almost altogether. Instead, I'd wander around the outskirts of the school, watching from afar. I usually found the spot behind the amphitheatre was the best. It was over the lip of the hill, so nobody could see over it. I'd bring a book to read or simply lay back on the soft grass and stare up at the sky.

Sometimes I'd see Tony walking around the field with his followers. He'd made a lot of new friends, but funnily enough, they were all from Charlene's gang of girls. I wondered how he could be so effortless, so confident. He could walk up to anyone and talk to them. He followed Charlene around like a lost puppy. I have to say, it bothered me. There were so many girls in the school, why did he pick her?

Bree had her own thing going on, too. She just joined the magazine club and was the head writer and editor. She'd spend all her free time at the IT suite writing 'hard-hitting' articles. She didn't seem to have much time for me anymore.

All signs of anything mysterious seemed to have all but vanished. There wasn't anything to investigate, so what was my purpose now?

There I was, sitting in my zone of comfort, minding my own business, when I was rudely interrupted...

'Excuse me.' A timid, familiar voice came from the ether.

I peeked over the top of my book. It was Charlene. She smiled so warmly it could have melted the polar ice caps. My heart almost packed up and left my chest.

I looked around. *Is she talking to me?*

I felt Phobos awakening, preparing for their attack.

'No, she was talking to the flowers,' they said witlessly.

I cleared my throat. 'Y-yes, that's me.' What a ridiculous reply. It didn't even make sense.

She laughed. 'Yes, I can see that.'

I leapt to my feet, brushing the dead grass off my trousers.

Without warning, the earth turned to quicksand beneath me. I sank slowly, inch by inch. Blades of grass wrapped around my ankles like rope, pulling me further down. I began to talk at a quicker pace before my waist completely vanished underground.

'So, what-uh, what brings you to me—here?' I clumsily tripped over the words.

She pulled the sleeves of her jumper over her hands. She seemed anxious to tell me something. She kept looking over her shoulder like she didn't want to be seen.

'I know you have that mystery thing. Tony told me all about it,' she said.

'Oh, that thing? Ha. That's dumb. It's for babies.'

'I think it's interesting.'

'Oh, yeah, no, I think that too!'

I was now almost up to my neck in mud.

Phobos could barely contain themselves. I could hear them slap their forehead. Despite this, Charlene kept on smiling politely. She walked closer to me, and with each step, my heart bounced faster around my chest.

'I wanted to tell you. I found something.'

'You f-found something?' I repeated.

'I didn't see it. I just heard it.'

I was intrigued. My curiosity caused me to forget about the ground swallowing me up.

'Do you think it's ... alien?' I asked.

She paused for thought. 'I'm not sure what it was. But you believe me, right?'

'I believe you. One hundred percent.'

Her hazel eyes lit up with pure joy.

The direction had changed; now my body began rising from my earthy prison.

Phobos got desperate. *'No, no, this isn't right! You're going to mess up sooner or later.'*

I ignored their pleas.

I was completely out of the ground now and eye level with her.

'So how come y-you're telling me this? What about Tony?'

'Well ... He ... Oh, this is stupid.' She sighed. 'Tony. Come out!'

From behind the grassy walls of the amphitheatre, Tony appeared. His head was hung low. He slowly walked over to us, stubbornly kicking the gravel as he went.

I couldn't stand to look at him. I thought Charlene had come here to see me by herself. But clearly it had all been a ruse to bring us together again.

'Hey ...' Tony said.

I stood with my back to him, arms folded. I could hear

Charlene quietly arguing with him in the background.

'I guess ... I'm sorry or something,' he said.

I turned to face him. I'd never heard him apologise for anything before. He didn't even say sorry for missing my birthday party. But he did buy me a basketball to make up for it. Even though I had never played basketball in my life.

'AHEM.' Charlene coughed forcefully.

Tony threw up his arms like saying sorry was the most difficult thing in the world.

'I'm sorry, OK! I'm sorry I got mad. I just thought you didn't want me there.'

I wasn't good at holding grudges or being in uncomfortable situations. 'It's OK,' I said.

Tony tilted his head. I guess I didn't sound totally convincing.

'So this thing you heard. Is that ... really real?' I asked.

Charlene nodded.

'You might want to get Bree first,' Tony said.

⌇

WE APPROACHED THE IT SUITE. Bree was sitting at her usual spot. She was completely locked in, typing away at a frightening pace. 'Hey, Bree!'

'Just a second,' she replied, holding up a finger.

'She's kind of a genius,' I whispered to Charlene.

'Oh,' she mouthed.

'But, you know, I'm kind of smart too,' I added.

Bree swivelled her chair around and faced us. She was startled. I assumed because it was shocking to see me talk with anyone other than her and Tony.

She extended her hand. 'Hi, I'm Bree. I don't think we've ever talked before ...'

Charlene smiled. 'No, but Tony talks about you a lot.'

Bree blushed a little. 'Oh?'

'Well, not "a lot", but, yeah, I told her you're a writer,' Tony said, slightly uneasy.

Bree turned and gestured to her monitor. There was a bunch of dots and dashes on the screen, with letters underneath.

'What's that?' I asked.

'Nothing. Well, I'm just trying to figure something out. You remember the'—she looked over my shoulder at Charlene, then lowered her voice—'UFO?'

'Obviously ...'

'Well, I think it might have been trying to communicate with us. And I might be able to figure out—'

'You guys wanna hear about this thing or what?' Tony blurted out.

Bree stopped and leant forward in her chair.

'Tell her ...' Tony said.

Charlene stepped forward. 'I heard this noise. It's hard to say. It's like a washing machine that's stuck under the floor.' Her voice trembled slightly.

'Where?' Bree asked.

∼

'WHY ARE WE BACK HERE?' I asked Charlene.

We were back at the amphitheatre. She led us around and into the centre of the circular-shaped theatre. Our shoes crunched beneath us. The ground was covered in gravel, with grass that poked out between the pieces of stone. Something had changed. The ground had been disturbed as if some colossal force had moved the earth and dug under it.

Charlene stopped dead in the centre. 'Here.'

Bree shrugged. 'I don't hear anything.'

'You have to go closer,' Tony said.

They crouched down and put their ears to the ground. Charlene waved, asking us to follow.

I bent down. As I got close, sure enough, I could hear an electronic humming. It whirred like an engine. The gravel vibrated. I shot up.

'What do you think is down there?' I asked.

'Could just be an earthquake,' Tony said, dismissing it.

'In England?' Charlene said, dumbfounded. 'Do we even have earthquakes?'

'Yeah, and tornados. I heard we get more tornados than any country in the world ...' Tony's voice trailed off.

As we discussed what horrors might be lurking below, I noticed that Bree's expression had changed. She had seen what the aliens were capable of. I had never seen her scared before, not from a horror movie, strict teachers, monsters, anything. She backed away from the epicentre and lifted herself up onto the grassy mound of the amphitheatre.

'Bree? You OK?' Tony asked.

'I'm fine. I need to finish that article by the end of today. The winner gets to write a story for the Gazette. You guys go ahead.'

She ran off across the playing field and back to the school building.

Tony looked totally stumped. He turned to me for help.

'I-I've gotta go practise,' I said hurriedly.

'For conkers?'

I nodded. 'Rematch is tomorrow.' I turned to head back when Tony said, 'Good luck.'

My gut was quivering just thinking about the rematch. But those two simple words actually gave me some comfort. 'Thank you.' I said.

14

THE REMATCH

The dance was only three weeks away; at least that'd be something to keep focused on, a goal at the end of the line. After that would be the sweet release of Christmas break, two weeks entirely school-free. Whatever the outcome of this conker fight was, at least I'd have that dance with Charlene. Thinking back, I hadn't even considered the two problems that would arise from this seemingly great deal.

1. I didn't know how to dance alone, never mind with other people.
2. How Tony would feel. What if he tried to strangle me?

My mediocre conker lay fizzing in the now-reeking pool of vinegar. I pinched my nose as I approached, picked it up, and studied it carefully. It didn't look any different.

Maybe it's stronger on the inside? I thought.

'Or maybe it's just a stinky piece of rubbish,' Phobos added helpfully.

It was too late at this point. All the best conkers were picked and smashed to pieces by now, this would have to do. I hurled my backpack over my shoulder and headed to school.

It was a particularly beautiful day; the sun was warming in the bitter autumn air. I smiled to myself as I walked. For the first time, it seemed like I couldn't lose, even if I did.

As I went through the steely gates, I felt the anticipation of our match. It seemed like everyone was watching me, as if Alex and I were the talk of the school.

Throughout English class I couldn't listen to a single word Miss Trigger said. Her words were like dissipating rain on my ears. All I could think about was the rematch. The missing boys, the beast in the woods, the UFO, all of it was now just background noise. Maybe this was a sign that I was meant to be popular. Maybe—

'Will! Are you with us?' Ms Trigger had me in her sights.

She probably noticed my glazed-over eyes looking vacantly out the window.

'Idiot,' someone cried out.

'Look at his face! It's bright red,' said another.

I squirmed on the carpet. The rough bristles scratched my legs.

'You can review chapter eleven for us,' Ms Trigger suggested.

Usually, I would ask Bree for the answer in emergency situations such as this, but she was on the far side of the circle. Phobos wasn't any use, either. I puffed out my chest and announced with confidence, 'I didn't finish reading the chapter, Ms Trigger.'

Ms Trigger was stunned into silence. It's not often students would be so truthful with a teacher.

'W-well, I'm glad you were honest with me, but next time, read it or you *will* fall behind in class.'

She continued the lesson and that was it. I expected a harsh response, maybe even detention, but nothing. Huh. I guess telling the truth isn't so bad. It's easier than lying, and it feels better too.

Anything to say? I asked Phobos. They didn't respond. *Guess not.*

~

TWELVE THIRTY P.M. Lunchtime. There was a soft patter of rain on the roof. It felt calming. I stood by the door, waiting to go out and face my opponent. Various matches were going on outside, dotted around the playground. I felt so unsure of myself. I had no one to cheer me on. I could have asked Bree or Tony to come, but I couldn't bear for them to see me fail. Again.

I gripped the door handle, wanting to turn it, but I knew there'd be no return once I did.

'Hey!' A voice cried out from the corridor.

I turned around and saw Charlene standing there with a big grin on her face. That was enough to light me up again.

'You're not going to lunch?' she asked.

'I was ... I am. There's something I have to do first.'

She must have detected fear in my voice, and she put a reassuring hand on my shoulder. I blushed a little.

'Well, good luck.'

I smiled. 'Thanks. Do you ... want to come watch?'

'Sure. Oh, and thank you.'

'For what?'

'For believing me.'

I smiled half-cocked and turned the handle. The door squeaked open.

The freezing droplets of rain splashed on my arm, and a shudder darted up and down my spine. *'I'm here when you lose, and you will lose,'* Phobos whispered in my ear.

I approached Alex, and the huge crowd gathered around him. I could easily spot him, of course; he was a foot taller than everyone else. The poor victim he was playing was out of sight, but I could hear them sobbing already.

I sighed and went to go in when Charlene grabbed my arm. 'It's just a game,' she said.

I could barely muster a smile. I pushed my way through the crowd. As I squeezed through excitable students, I could hear them spreading rumours about Alex's previous victims.

'I heard he broke a Year 3 kid's arm.'

'Is it true? He knocked out Greg's front teeth?'

I gulped and wondered if I should go on. Alex was standing there with his arms folded and chin held high, like he was waiting for me. 'You ready for round two?' he asked, peering down his nose at me.

I looked back at where I'd come from. I'd lost sight of Charlene.

'Y-yup.'

We let our conkers fall to our sides. A familiar face came out from the crowd and approached us.

'Huh? What are you doing here?' I asked.

'I'm the referee,' Tony said, winking at me.

An odd smell arose from below. It was the vinegar. It started to waft up into the nostrils of poor unsuspecting students. Alex held his nose and contorted his face. 'What is that smell?'

Everyone in the crowd sniffed the air and pulled the

same expression. I had to think quickly to save embarrassment. 'Hmm. It must be the canteen food.'

Tony stuck his arm in between us both to start the game. 'Winner goes first.' He snatched his arm back again.

Without hesitation, Alex drew back his conker and struck mine with a heavy blow. Was this all for nothing? Had Grandma's method failed? Maybe I hadn't left it in the vinegar long enough. I looked down.

Not a single scratch!

There was a collective gasp from the crowd. Alex was stunned. He couldn't believe it.

Tony pointed towards me. 'Player Two, it's your turn.'

I didn't take any chances this time. I aimed carefully, closing one eye to focus on the target. I swung down and smacked it left of the middle. I opened the other eye to assess the damage. There was a large crack in his conker.

The crowd gasped again, then fell eerily quiet. This unnerved me more than the shouting and cheering. The pressure felt immense. Alex raised his conker again, but Tony grabbed his arm. 'Wait for my signal.'

He shook Tony off and grunted like a pig. Tony looked back at me and winked. *What is he doing? Is this part of some plan I wasn't aware of?*

'OK, Player One, take your turn.'

Alex swung again, even more furiously, and struck mine almost directly down the middle.

No damage.

'What is this? What did you do?' Alex demanded. The veins in his forehead were practically popping out.

I shrugged and shook my head. 'I-I don't know, honestly.'

The crowd grew louder again. I felt like they were about to turn on me, like a horde of zombies.

'Go, Will!' I heard in the distance. It was Charlene. She was watching me from the edges of the ever-growing crowd.

'Yeah, go, Will, smash him to pieces!' yelled another.

A girl appeared by my side; it was Bree. 'You've got this.'

Tony signalled in my direction. 'Player Two, when you're ready.'

Alex snatched his conker away before I could do anything. 'No, you're playing a trick. You weirdos did something!'

The crowd began to turn on him. 'Boo!'

There aren't words big enough to describe the rush of energy I felt. The stars had aligned, the tables had turned, and for once in my short life, I just knew I was going to win. I was so sure of myself.

Alex kept yanking the string away. Tony grabbed it firmly and told him, 'You play until there's a winner.'

He reluctantly gave in and hung the conker out for the final time. The crowd simmered down, waiting for the next hit. I flicked the conker over my finger, the string tight against my fist, and rained it down with such power it obliterated his into a million pieces. The debris scattered like an exploding star.

Everyone went into a crazy hysteria, like I'd just won the World Cup. They jumped up and down, causing a mini earthquake. I wanted to duck out of there as soon as possible. As much as I savoured the victory, I hated being the centre of attention. So, I slunk out through the crowd, students patting me on the back and chanting my name as I went. I could faintly hear Alex raging in the background. As my thoughts turned inwards, I thought about Charlene's words of wisdom. *It's just a game.* But that didn't make winning any less sweet.

Bree ran up and smothered me in a bear hug. Tony

slapped me on the back. It stung. Sometimes I wondered if he knew his own strength.

'Thank you, really, I mean it, but I want to be alone right now.'

They stopped me in my tracks. 'No, not this time, mate,' Tony insisted. 'We're celebrating, my treat.'

I looked back to catch Alex storming off into the school, his face still frozen in shock.

'I don't get it. My conker didn't even have a scratch,' I said.

'Maybe your grandma's trick worked,' Tony hurriedly answered.

'Yeah, I guess ... Wait. How do you know about that?'

Tony tried sneaking away, but I stopped him.

'Well, your mum still talks to my mum. She said you were doing some experiment in your room and it stank of vinegar.'

'I guess that makes sense.'

Bree ran over to the IT suite. 'Bye, guys, I need to write this down while it's fresh!' We waved her goodbye.

'You hungry?' Tony asked.

'Starving.'

15

THE CANTEEN

W e headed to the canteen. The whole place was heaving with students. Fridays were extra special because they served cheeseburgers. They became so popular they would sell out in under ten minutes. It quickly became a chance for low-level scoundrels, who snuck out of class earlier to line up for them. They would order four or five, then sell them to awaiting students outside, for double the cost, of course.

We saw Charlene across the hall, chatting with her friends. They kept looking over at me. I averted my eyes. Tony watched them from afar.

'I guess you wanna hang out with your friends now, huh?' I asked.

He punched my arm playfully. 'Nah. I think I'll hang out with the conker champion, if that's cool with you ...'

'Oh. It might be.' I beamed with happiness.

We ordered drinks and a cone of chips to share. We plonked ourselves down at the usual spot in the corner, away from potential conversation with strangers. I saw several popular kids pass us by. They all nodded and acknowledged us. *Are we popular now?* This felt too good to be true.

We'd nearly finished our lunch when we were approached by the football boys. Alex was with them but stayed near the back, hanging his head in shame. Nick sat down opposite us. He bought Charlene along with him. She seemed uncomfortable as she squirmed in her seat. Tony curled his fists and shook.

'I heard you did good today,' Nick said. He grabbed a handful of our chips and stuffed his face. 'A little too good.'

I suddenly lost my appetite.

'So how does a little kid like you beat someone like that?' He gestured over at Alex. Our eyes met, but he quickly looked away.

'Because he's a big idiot!' Phobos yelled.

I wanted to say it out loud so badly.

'You boys seen Thomas and Dave around?' Nick said out of nowhere.

I spurted juice out my nose. It wasn't pretty. The orange liquid ran out my nostrils and dribbled onto my plate.

The football boys recoiled in disgust.

'N-n-n ...' I couldn't say it. I couldn't lie.

'Yes! The UFO took them away!' Phobos laughed.

'No, we haven't,' Tony said. His voice was firm and steady.

Nick produced a tissue from his pocket and dabbed his cheek. He delicately wiped Charlene's chin too. At this point he was just rubbing it in.

'Hmm,' he said. 'Anyway, Alex told me about your deal.'

Tony turned his attention to me with great suspicion. Nick noticed this and grinned madly. 'Oh, he hasn't told you about the deal?'

My head felt like it might catch fire any second now. My stomach bubbled, and my toes curled.

'Just to let you know, the deal's off.' Nick stood up. He wrapped his arm around Charlene. She looked like a mouse caught in a cat's claws.

Before he walked away, he added one final log to the fire. 'I'm surprised. I thought you boys were best friends.'

With that, they made their exit.

Tony now had his full attention on me.

'I g-guess I should head to class now.' I said.

'What was that about? What deal?' Tony asked.

'It's Nick. He's just messing around like he always does.'

Tony breathed in deeply and out again. At least he was trying to calm himself down. I'd rather not be caught in one of his tantrums.

'Tell me,' he said in between laboured breaths. 'did something happen to them? Thomas and Dave?'

'I c-can't tell you.'

Tony sprung up from his chair and stormed through the canteen, knocking over chairs and food trays as he went.

That could have gone a lot worse.

It was clear that Alex had been toying with me all along. He could have never promised me a dance with Charlene. He wanted to give me hope, to humiliate me. I was beginning to suspect the boys knew the truth about Thomas and Dave. After all, I was the last person they saw them with.

16

AUDITIONS

Before the end of the school year, the drama teacher picks an exciting play or musical to adapt. They're usually amateur-looking and extremely cheap, but the parents love it. My dad would use any excuse to use his brand-new camcorder.

Now it's a little cliché, as the quiet kid, but I always ended up playing the tree. It might be seen as an insult, as if we're not good enough at acting or singing. So we simply play a dead piece of wood standing at the back of the stage. I didn't mind it one bit. It meant I could blend in unseen whilst getting to enjoy the play. Also, I wouldn't have the embarrassment of forgetting my lines or hitting a note off-key.

This year's choice was *Space Explorers: The Musical*. Now, there was a small problem here. None of us knew what *Space Explorers* was. That didn't seem to matter, though. Any excuse to make costumes and dress as aliens was fine by us.

We all sat in a line along the benches in the school hall. Ms Chambers, the drama teacher, was the director. She wore a suit jacket and tall high heels. She tapped her finger against her lips, studying the class, picking out her chosen stars.

'Firstly, we need a Blaze Nova. He must be strong, confident, a great leader.' She scanned us again. Her finger pointed at Nick. He perked up like a meerkat.

'Hmm. No, no, he must be able to sing.' I could tell that stung him deeply. His shoulders drooped. That felt satisfying. I looked around to seek Tony's approval, but he ignored me completely. He was focused on Charlene, who was practically sitting in Nick's lap.

'You.' Ms Chambers wagged her finger at Benny, an unexpected choice.

Benny stood up and immediately began belting out Robbie Williams's 'Angels'. It was bizarre, but he actually sounded good! The class giggled.

'Right, we have our Blaze! Next, Mr. Kluge. He's nerdy and a bit of a know-it-all.'

She didn't even hesitate as she pointed out Bree in the crowd. 'Perfect.'

Bree looked bewildered but flattered she was chosen. 'Do you want me to sing?'

'No, no need.'

Bree looked disappointed but accepted it anyway.

'Finally, we need our Astrid. She's a tough, intelligent pilot.

A hand shot up a few rows in front of me.

'OK, do you have the pipes?' Ms Chambers asked.

Charlene stood up and sung some haunting old-timey song I hadn't heard before. I was entranced. She had a beautiful, delicate singing voice. Everyone was hushed into silence.

'Well, there's my answer.'

Charlene sat down and glanced back at me, flashing a

grin. I stuck my thumbs up and offered an awkward smile in return. *'You're so lame,'* Phobos said.

Nick noticed this. I quickly changed my smile into a frown and pretended to look elsewhere.

As the roles began to dwindle, almost everyone was picked. Last up was Tony and me. I was worried. I didn't think there were any trees in space. I would have to do something 'real' this time.

Ms Chambers snapped her fingers. 'I got it. You two are astronauts—'

I guess that's pretty cool, I thought.

'—and you're going to come out after each scene and tell a joke to the audience.'

Was that a common thing in *Space Explorers*? I didn't realise it was a comedy.

'Both of you work together and make some jokes ready for the play.'

My insides turned sour, and I grabbed my chest in pain. *'You're not funny,'* Phobos said. *'And Tony is the most serious person you know.'*

I scanned the room to find Tony, but he was already looking directly at me. He gave me daggers: a look that could pierce diamonds. This was going to be tricky.

17

THE GARAGE

My mum pranced around the living room in pure joy. She couldn't be happier about my starring role.

'Next stop, Hollywood,' Dad said sarcastically from behind his newspaper.

I rolled my eyes and played it off like it was no big deal. James made a rare appearance from the gaming den to see what all the fuss was about.

'Your brother has a big acting role in the school musical.' Mum squealed.

'OK,' he said, closing the door shut again. That was pretty much the reaction I expected.

'You need a costume.'

'No, Mum, I—'

Before I could finish my sentence, she began rummaging around in her box of fabrics and textiles. She had a treasure trove of costumes she'd made for me and James.

Last year we went to the school fayre as a pair of jesters. Admittedly, we looked great, with a hat, bell, and everything. Sadly, Alex tore the shirt sleeves, saying, "I'm just joking," as he did it. But I never told Mum. It'd break her heart.

She stood back and assessed the situation. 'Hmm, no, no we need something shiny.'

Another light bulb flashed over her head, and she ran into the kitchen.

'So, you're an astronaut then?' Dad asked, flipping over a page in his newspaper.

'Yep.'

Mum burst from the kitchen with armfuls of tin foil. She let them roll over the floor.

'Now, we just need a helmet.'

Dad lowered his newspaper. 'Should still have the old motorcycle helmet in the garage.'

'Oh, yeah!'

I faced Dad, confused. 'You ... had a motorbike?'

He suddenly perked up. 'Oh yeah, your mum and I would ride around all the time. Triumph T140. Cost us an arm and a leg. We went everywhere, didn't we, love?'

Mum beamed and blushed a little, clearly remembering their youth.

'You were cool?' I asked.

Dad laughed and grabbed his chest like I just shot him. 'Still am,' he said, winking at Mum.

I started feeling a little sick.

'Can you go find the helmet, Will? Key's hanging by the door,' she said.

I poked my head into the gaming den. 'James. Come help me in the garage.'

'Why?' he said, as he kept on button-mashing the controller.

'Just come! We could look for your old RC Monster Truck.'

He reluctantly paused his game and followed me outside.

The wind lapped our faces as we walked away from the warm confines of the house. To be honest, I invited James because I was afraid of the garage. It was creepy and extremely dark.

We slotted the key inside the lock of the creaky old door. It swung open. I always hated this part. I would reach around the inside of the wall to flick on the light switch. I felt if I took too long to turn it on, a long gangly arm would reach out of the shadows and grab me. Light was my ally; nothing could touch me in the light. In the wide-open doorway, I stared into the void for a long time.

James nudged me in the ribs. 'Hurry up, it's cold!'

I reached for the light switch and felt the sticky webbing of a spider's web. I lurched back and let out a pathetic tiny scream. James sighed and went in first. The dusty old light bulb flickered into life. The place was filled with clutter. Some of it was Dad's tools, and others were ancient toys we didn't play with anymore. I scanned the workshop table and blew away the layer of dust and filth. I noticed a pair of wire-cutters hanging on the wall.

'Are you kidding me?' I laughed to myself.

We couldn't find the helmet anywhere. 'Maybe it's at the back,' James suggested.

I hesitated. The back of the garage was covered in darkness. The light couldn't reach there. 'You go look.' I prodded James in the back. Real hero I was.

He steadily disappeared into the shadows. I could hear a slight rustling. The outlines of boxes wobbling. 'James, are you doing that?' I asked, my voice quivering.

I got no response. All I could hear was the patter of feet moving across the floor.

'J-James,'

A silhouette emerged from the shadows, but the light blocked my vision. It had a gigantic head and a tiny body. I covered my eyes and began to tremble.

'Got it,' said a tiny voice.

I lowered my hands. James was wearing the oversized helmet over his head. He had a huge, cheeky grin on his face. I shoved him. 'Why didn't you say anything?'

'Funny,' he said.

CRASH!

A pile of boxes tumbled to the ground. Strange chittering noises arose from the back of the garage. James immediately leapt behind me. I put out my arms to shield him.

'Y-you heard that, right?' I asked.

He nodded, I think, but I couldn't peel my eyes away.

A pair of tiny greenish/silverish feet poked out from the shadows. They had only two toes. The rest of the body was hidden, except the eyes. The eyes were lit like beacons, giving out a white reflection from the pupils. They darted up and down, clearly studying us.

I slowly reached behind us, feeling around the wall. There it was. I grabbed the wire-cutters and pointed them at the creature. My hands were shaking wildly. I couldn't hold them out for long.

It studied the sharp edges with great interest. It reached out its spindly arms and poked the edge of the blade. It screeched—a horrible sound like nails on a chalkboard. I had heard that sound before. It was the same awful screams of pain I had heard coming from the barn. It retracted its arm and shuffled back into the darkness.

I realised I was scaring it. I slowly set the wire-cutters

down and pushed them to one side, showing I was no longer a threat.

The creature stepped out again into the light. I could see it clearer now. It looked like a human baby, only with freakishly long arms and stubby legs. Its head was oval-shaped, with no ears, eyelashes, anything. Only two small black eyes.

It dawned on me that this thing must be the alien. The pilot from the UFO. It was roughly the same size as the cockpit, plus it certainly wasn't any kind of animal I'd ever seen before.

I crouched down to its level.

'F-friend,' I said, pointing at my chest.

The alien cocked its head. It moved in quick, twitchy movements, like a small bird.

'Friend,' I repeated, pointing at it.

The lack of responses unsettled us.

The light bulb that swung above our heads dimmed. The room was quickly cast into darkness. At first, I thought it was the alien. Perhaps it had killed the power, like the UFO had before. But no, that horrible, slippery voice came back.

'Listen carefully, coward,' Phobos said. *'This thing could help us. Go on, ask it.'*

I gulped, then took a step forwards. The alien lurched back. I put out my hands and crouched down slowly. I was careful not to make any sudden movements.

As I got closer, more details became clear to me. There were burn marks around its neck, like it had been shocked by electricity or something.

'Did he hurt you? The farmer?' I asked.

It cocked its head.

'We're good people. Me and my brother. We won't hurt you, right, James?'

James made an inhuman noise. He was useless.

I turned to the alien again and relayed Phobos's words.

'Can ... help? Can you help us?'

The alien stopped jittering. It just stared at me with those lifeless black eyes.

'You could ask him to take away those bullies ...' Phobos's words dripped into my ears like poison. *'Not to hurt them. Just take them away someplace.'*

I couldn't. I wouldn't. What kind of person would I be? The first human contact with a real-life alien and they ask them to do something terrible. I was an explorer, a researcher. No, I couldn't do it ...

James was so frightened he backed into the workshop table by accident, causing Dad's tools to drop to the floor. They clanged and clinked and made an awful racket.

The noise spooked the alien so much that it spun around sharply and ran for the garage door. It unhooked the latch and lifted it up so fast the door hit the top and shook the entire building. Just like that, it was gone.

We took a second to catch our breath. James spun me around and peered into my eyes with equal parts fear and wonder.

I held him at arm's length. 'Are you OK?'

'It was watching us,' he said calmly.

His words chilled me to the core.

It was.

18

TREMORS

Tony and I spent the next couple of weeks working together on our act in our quiet spot behind the amphitheatre. He wasn't exactly fun to work with. His mood had turned sour ever since learning about 'the deal'. I could tell he wanted to ask about it, but perhaps he already knew the answer. It didn't matter anyway. The dance with Charlene was off.

He studied our script with a look of doubt. 'Are you sure that's funny?' he asked.

I was fiddling with the patch of daisies next to me. 'Read it to me again.'

He cleared his throat. 'OK, ahem. Why couldn't the star stay focused?'

'I don't kn—'

'He kept spacing out.'

Neither of us laughed.

'I think you should leave a gap in the middle,' I suggested.

'Huh?'

'Well, you kind of said the last part really quickly.'

He scoffed at my advice. 'I don't know, I've never told jokes before!'

Bree skipped over to us with a prideful look on her face. 'Hey, guys.' She sat down beside us.

'Greetings, Mr Kluge.' We giggled.

She didn't change her expression one bit. She wasn't about to let us rain on her parade. 'How's your script going?' she asked.

Tony threw his pencil down in frustration.

'Oh, that bad?'

I leant over and whispered to her. 'I think we need your help. We don't know how to be funny.'

Bree tilted her head back and laughed hard. She had to hold her sides from the pain. 'That's what you're worried about?'

'Laugh all you want!' Tony snapped.

'See, you are funny!'

I stared off into the distance.

Bree pulled herself together, wiping tears away. 'Anyway, you got any more news for me? Any sightings?'

Tony ripped out a handful of grass. 'Nah, haven't seen nothing.'

I collected my thoughts for a minute. *Should I tell them? They're going to know straight away—they know I can't lie.*

'Will? Have you seen anything?' she asked.

Oh no.

'You better shut up; you're good at that,' Phobos said.

I decided to go against their advice. 'I … James and me. We saw something in our garage.'

Bree perked up and grabbed her notepad, seemingly from thin air. Tony's face dropped.

'Was it a Code Fifty-Two?'

'No, Code Fifty-Three.'

She let go of her notepad in shock. 'It was ... extra-terrestrial?'

'It was an alien, yeah,' I confirmed.

Tony laughed bitterly. 'Hah.'

'Just ignore him,' Bree said. 'Did you get a good look at it?'

'I just saw its eyes. They were black. Its pupils were white. It only had two toes.'

Bree shuddered from the description.

'Did it say anything?' she asked.

'No, it ran away.'

'Oh, that's convenient, isn't it?' Tony blurted out.

I ignored him again.

Bree grabbed my arm. 'You think it's the pilot from the UFO?'

'I think so ...'

Tony stood up impatiently. 'I'm going to clear my head.' He took off down the slope and began jogging around the amphitheatre.

'Will'—Bree caught my gaze, and her tone turned serious—'where do you think it went?'

I paused, then said, 'It could be anywhere.'

JUST THEN, a flock of birds scattered in the blue sky above us. The ground grumbled and growled like we were sitting on a giant's belly. Tony lost his balance and fell onto the gravel. His hands went out first, scraping and scratching his palms. Bree and I had to steady ourselves as the wobbling earth nearly sent us tumbling down the hill.

'That was stronger!' Bree said.

The shaking gradually slowed down and we regained

our balance. The dust settled and the sounds of chirping birds returned.

'Are you OK?' I shouted down at Tony.

He scowled. 'Fine. Must be another aftershock.'

'That was no aftershock,' Phobos said. *'You know it. I know it. It's something way bigger.'*

19

SPACE EXPLORERS

The night before showtime, I lay in bed with thoughts racing and crashing around in my head. Phobos was having a field day. He enjoyed drilling these negative thoughts into me.

I stared at the starry sky above. Usually, they sent me into a blank space where I could relax and be alone with my thoughts. This time, I didn't want to be alone with my thoughts, I wanted to escape from them.

I wrenched my eyes closed once again. When they opened, it was performance night. I was standing in front of a big poster at the school reception. It read:

SPACE EXPLORERS: THE MUSICAL.
ONE NIGHT ONLY.

Mum and Dad stood beside me, ushering me inside. 'You ready, kiddo?' Dad said giddily.

I didn't respond.

I'd already reached the stage where I blanked everything out, and my mouth was sewn shut.

Mum and Dad went to sit with the other parents, and I went backstage with all the other students. Everyone was changing into their costumes.

Bree ran over to me, makeup half finished. One eyebrow was painted upwards, and the other normal, so it looked like she was highly suspicious of something. I snorted at her strange appearance. It felt good to laugh. It released some steam.

'Can you help me with my lines?' Bree asked hurriedly. She handed me her laminated script.

'Um, don't we go on stage in ten minutes?'

She snatched the script back. 'Forget it! I need to get changed.'

I spotted Charlene in the makeup chair. I gave her an awkward little wave in the mirror. She smiled. 'Hey, you ready for the show?' I asked.

'I was born ready,' she boasted.

I didn't know what to say next. I wasn't used to talking with confident people. 'Aren't you ... nervous?'

'No. Why? Are you?'

'No ... Well, sometimes.' I scratched the nape of my neck.

'I'm just kidding! Yeah, I'm a little nervous.'

I breathed a sigh of relief. She was a normal person, after all.

'How many people out there now?' she asked.

I parted the curtains to peek out. There was an unholy number of parents filling every seat.

'Just a few.'

I think I was trying to convince myself more than anything.

Ms Chambers threw open the curtains and badgered all the lingering students. 'Positions, everyone!'

We all scattered around, hoisting the spaceship set into place, fixing the cardboard backdrops onto the wall. 'Five Minutes. We. Are. Go.' She clapped.

My eyes widened in fear. *The costume!* I quickly pulled up the costume box and shuffled on the trousers and sweatshirt. The foil was peeling off. I patted it down again, but the edges were splitting open. *The helmet. Where's the helmet?*

I emptied the entire box, but it wasn't there. I felt lightheaded. Mum would be utterly destroyed. She worked so hard on it. Benny passed by in his Blaze Nova costume. I ran up to him.

'H-hey, Benny. Have you seen my helmet?'

He put his hand on my shoulder sympathetically. 'Sorry, mate, haven't seen it.'

The panic was setting in.

'Ten. Nine. Eight. Seven. Six. Five.' Ms Chambers counted down.

I ran frantically to my position at the back.

'Four. Three. Two. One.'

The curtains raised, and the white stage lights immediately seared my eyes. I was the last student in place. Looking out over the crowd, all I could make out was a sea of nameless faces. They all appeared as blurs of shapes and colours. A large array of blinking red lights along with them. There had to be over a hundred video cameras there. I spotted Mum and Dad sitting near the middle. They gave me a thumbs-up, although Mum looked concerned at my missing costume piece.

SCENE ONE:

Benny and Bree sat on a wooden box, pretending to be steering the ship through a perilous asteroid field. We all tilted side to side, like we were shifting gravity.

'The Blorbons are gaining on us, Captain,' said Charlene, pressing buttons on a crudely painted cardboard computer.

Benny smiled cockily. 'They'll try. Hit it!' He slid the joystick to maximum speed.

Bree pulled her hair in frustration. 'But, sir, the odds of surviving are 481,516 to 1!'

Ms Chambers mouthed along to the words. She smugly watched on as if she had created an award-winning masterpiece.

As the scene finished, the audience clapped and whooped. I felt the disaster coming; it was unfolding in my mind like a car crash. It was time to be funny.

When you are in the spotlight, it seems like time stops completely. Every breath, every sound becomes increasingly heightened. You become very aware of the sound of your own voice, and it becomes difficult to project it past a tiny squeak. The pressure to be funny, to be interesting, or worth other people's time feels like it wouldn't be worth saying anything. At least, in my mind. But here I was. It would be better to say something than nothing at all.

SCENE TWO:

I started hopping on each leg, sticking out my arms like I was floating through the air. I eyed Tony on the other side. We met in the middle of the stage. I shut my eyes, memorising the jokes one last time. I opened them again, and something horrifying lay before me. Tony was wearing my helmet. He smiled at me, unfazed. I couldn't believe it. This was a betrayal on another level.

'You're a terrible astronaut,' Tony said.

The audience murmured.

Huh? This wasn't in the script, I thought.

He turned to address the audience directly. 'He hasn't got a helmet in space ... how is he alive?'

There were a few scattered laughs. He delivered with such seriousness the crowd wasn't sure whether to laugh or not. I turned so red; I might have been mistaken for a tomato.

I could detect Phobos slinking his way into my thoughts.

'He's been a bad friend. Let him have it,' he silkily spoke into my ear.

I shoved the script into my trouser pocket.

'Well maybe if you'd remembered to pack it, I would be alive!'

The audience broke out into laughter. Maybe this could work to my advantage.

I looked over at Ms Chambers. She was flipping furiously through script pages. Then, rather abruptly, things turned ugly.

'What is this deal with the football boys?' he demanded.

I knew that was coming. I turned my back to him, and the audience, desperately searching for an escape. But the exits were gone. The doors had vanished. I was surrounded by 4 solid walls and a sea of cameras.

Tony reached out and turned me around. 'Don't ignore me like you ignore everyone else.'

That fired me up, but I refused to budge. The audience's laughter began dying down, replaced with worried whispers.

'Let me tell you something.' He backed up, ready to unload some uncomfortable truths. 'You cheated at that conkers game.'

The students gasped! Some of them booed like at an old-timey pantomime.

'What? No I didn't.' I scoffed.

'You did! You put the conker in vinegar to make it stronger.'

The football boys glared at us. Alex smashed his fists together.

'T-that's not cheating. E-everybody does it.'

'No they don't.'

I couldn't handle the shame. Was I a cheater? I didn't even know what I did was wrong. But what hurt most of all was this coming from the lips of my own supposed best friend.

The embarrassment bubbled up, but my anger took over and continued to well up inside until it was ready to burst from the temples.

'Well, I was going to dance with Charlene at the winter dance!' I yelled.

The air turned sour. Charlene slunk in her chair until she disappeared. Everyone turned to look at her. I guess she didn't know about the deal. Tony clutched his fists. I took a step backwards.

'That was the deal? You *know* I like her.'

I had to choose my next words wisely, but I was a child of poor decisions.

'Well, you should have asked her first.'

With that, I saw a crazed Tony rush at me. We tussled for a bit, then smashed into the 'spaceship' walls. They came crashing down. All the students were in fits of laughter. The audience was appalled. I even heard a few screams. Ms Chambers had collapsed to the floor in despair. It wasn't long before we were fighting for real, and the laughter died down.

It took several parents to pull us apart. We were caught up in the velvet stage curtains and pieces of cardboard. Luckily for me, Tony's helmet blocked his vision, so he didn't manage to get many decent hits on me. And luckily for Tony, my arms were as thin as noodles and equally as effective as weapons.

Outside the school, everyone went to their cars, chatting about the eventful musical. It was freezing cold. Mum and Dad were stunned. I think they were actively trying to erase their minds of what they had just seen. I was attempting to do the same.

'I don't think your drama teacher has seen *Space Explorers*,' Dad said, trying to cut the tension with a dull knife.

Mum didn't say a word. It was highly unusual for her. I knew this could only mean one thing: she was disappointed.

We travelled home in silence that night.

20

PARENTS' EVENING

There is nothing on this earth more terrifying than parents' evening. Honestly, I would have preferred to be mauled by a lion rather than attend this miserable event.

To those unaware, or lucky enough to never have suffered the misfortune, parents' evening is where you go to school after dark, walk around, and talk to any subject teacher your mum and dad wish to see. You must sit between them, facing your teacher directly, and you're torturously read all the little details about how well (or dreadfully unwell) you are performing in class.

It felt so weird being in school after dark, like seeing your teacher in a shopping centre—it's not natural. My stomach sunk into my shoes as we passed each classroom. My parents wanted to see each teacher I had.

First up, Mr Bennison. 'Hello, please, take a seat.'

My mum sat to my left, dressed in her finest clothes and makeup. She took these outings seriously. My dad sat to my right, dressed just as well as he could manage, in a stripy polo shirt and jeans. They listened intently to every word.

'I can see William is distracted by something. He doesn't appear to be showing much interest in science ...'

The words trailed off as I tried to go somewhere else in my mind. Anywhere was fine, just not here. Even Phobos was quiet—it was humiliating enough; they didn't even have to show up.

Next, Ms Moneagle.

'I think Will has a creative mind, but he's afraid to show it. He can be a little ... shy.'

'Shy,' Mr Litchford, the geography teacher added.

'Shy,' said Mr Bennison.

'Shy,' said Ms Chambers.

'Shy.'

'Shy.'

'Shy.'

I want to take a second to explain the word 'shy' and why I hate it so much. It's simply a lazy word. It's incredibly easy to label someone 'shy' when they don't speak up, participate in class, or hang out with friends very often.

Without truly knowing them, how do you really know how they feel on the inside? It's unimaginable to those who can easily speak with large groups of people or keep up friendships for long amounts of time. I'm not mad at them; in fact, I'm envious. How I wished to be like them.

I think it's a little like batteries. People make me tired. I need to go home and recharge. I like being alone. I mean, I like my friends, but even they can be too much sometimes. Too noisy. Other people don't seem to be like this. They enjoy the noisy. Maybe this charges them up.

Finally, we landed at Mrs Collings's classroom. You know what they say, save the best for last. Her weary eyes scowled at us from the moment we entered her office. I slowed my pace, as if making the walk over to her any slower would make it go away. Even my dad looked a little afraid.

'So'—she licked her finger, turning the page over in my file. She studied it with great scrutiny—'Will is performing, let's say, below average in class.'

Dad gave me the angriest stare you'd ever seen.

'As you know, he's had a few "incidents" over the last few months, and I think this newfound rebellious streak has caused him to lose sight of what's important.'

I wondered which 'incidents' she could have been speaking of. The missing boys? The bad test results? The fight in the musical?

Phobos was stirring.

'Also, Will needs to participate more in class. I think he's quite a shy boy.'

There's that word again.

Phobos was winding up, ready to pounce.

Maybe if you weren't such a scary teacher, I would talk more! I blurted out.

I sprang up and jumped onto her desk. The pencils and marker pens scattered and rolled over the edge.

You think being mean is a good way to make us behave? It only makes us hate you more.

She looked utterly shocked and grasped her chest as if to calm herself.

I want to be better. I want to talk and do well in maths and ... be normal. But I don't know how!

I began to sob uncontrollably, my words drowned by my tears.

'Will? Sweetheart? What's wrong?' Mum asked.

I was back in my chair, Mrs Collings's utensils untouched. I had definitely dreamed it this time. But I *was* crying. That part was real. Mum tried her best to console me, putting a reassuring hand on my shoulder. Dad did the same. Mrs Collings looked uncomfortable. She leant forward in her chair.

'Look, I don't wish to sound harsh, but it's important to be honest. There are positives and negatives to every student. They're still growing and figuring out who they are, so it's my job to help them along that path with the little time I have with them. I didn't say he was incapable; I said he needs to try, to prove he can do it.'

Mrs Collings's words didn't exactly make me feel better, but at least they were honest.

'As for the winter dance, I'm afraid I'll have to ban Will from attending.'

I stood up, wiping tears from my eyes. 'N-no, I-I have to go. Please. You c-can't.'

Dad sat me back down and told me to take a deep breath. I wished this was still a dream, but it was reality.

'I'm sorry, but there needs to be consequences for his actions.'

Just like that, the dream was over.

21

JAILBREAK

Nothing felt worth doing anymore. Tony and I hadn't spoken all week. And we were still recovering from our injuries. Mum tried to talk with his dad on the phone, but he refused to let us see each other.

The house was covered wall-to-wall in tinsel and fairy lights. This was Mum's time to shine, she loved to decorate for Christmas. It was only a week away, after all. I felt as though I didn't deserve happiness. I planned to stay in the gaming den for the duration of the holidays and shove my face with chocolate bars to numb the pain. The winter dance was two nights away, so I'd rather forget it even existed. I stared at the TV, mashing the buttons on my controller with no rhyme or reason. I took another swig from my Choco's tube. They'd all gone. I had officially hit rock bottom.

The TV signal cut out suddenly, and the white snowy screen began emitting a horrible high-pitched tone. It grew so loud I had to cover my ears.

SCRRRR!

It shut off. The screen went black. Only the white noise lingered.

'William.'

I shivered at the sound of Phobos's voice.

'Let's talk,' they said.

No. I hate you.

They made mocking crying noises as though I'd hurt their feelings. *'Ouch. Now you have no friends, not even me.'*

I shoved the sofa cushions against my ears to try to block their voice, but they sounded clearer than ever before.

Please go away.

'You really want to tell your only friend to go away?'

I threw the cushions back down. I was losing the battle, so I did something stupid; I listened to them.

'It's time to leave. Think about it. The family could save some money, no presents, food, clothes. Maybe it'd be best if they never had you in the first place.'

I couldn't find the strength to fight it. It seemed like there were no alternatives, and Phobos was the only 'friend' that gave me any options. So, I had to pick the right time to run away.

I hatched a daring escape plan. On Thursday evenings, Mum went to Zumba class (some fitness thing). Dad usually crashed on the sofa and watched TV. James would be in the gaming den, so naturally, he wouldn't notice if I were gone anyway. That gave me a rough two-hour window to get out.

That evening I crept downstairs and acted casual. Dad asked if I wanted any takeaway.

'I'll just make something in the kitchen,' I replied.

He shrugged and went back to watching reruns of *Off-Road Truckers*. In the kitchen, I grabbed my lunchbox and nabbed six slices of bread.

This'll be enough, I thought.

I made six cheese and onion sandwiches, crudely cut them into halves, and shoved the lunchbox inside my bag. I hoisted the bag over my shoulder, exited through the back door of the kitchen, and carefully tiptoed out the back garden gate.

I followed the same route I walked to school and diverted halfway. I took a deep breath and inhaled my new sense of freedom. I couldn't believe it; I was truly independent. Is this how it feels to be an adult? I could do this forever. I had food, warmth, and ... nowhere to go.

There was a fatal flaw in my plan. Where would I stay? I hadn't thought this through. I looked back down the long decrepit road. Home was only three streets away, but the roads started to stretch and contort into an endless valley.

'Now what, genius?' Phobos asked. *'You're going to freeze to death out here.'*

They made a good point.

I continued onwards and turned down a road I'd never been before. The houses were magnificent, old buildings with grand fixtures on the outside. *This must be where the rich families live.* I continued down the road. A pair of adults were walking right at me. I wanted to cross the street, but for some twisted reason, fear kept me on the path right towards them. As they approached, they grew to seven feet tall, spindly, and had twisted, demented smiles. They withdrew a book from their inner coat pocket.

'Hi!' the man said, waving his leather-gloved hand at me.

I was glued to the spot.

I heard a muffled 'Will!' coming from above.

I stared upwards at the gloomy sky. 'Hello?' I said.

There was banging on glass. I looked to my left, and there was Bree in the upstairs window. 'Stay there,' she said

The adults walked on past me, and I hurriedly ran to her

door. Her steps thudded down the stairs. The wait felt like forever.

Come on! Please hurry.

She yanked open the front door. 'Hey ... what are you doing here?'

She eyed my overstuffed backpack.

'Oh, I was just going for a walk,' I lied.

She grew even more suspicious. 'Well, it's almost zero degrees. Why don't you come in?'

I hesitated. If her family saw me, they might try to ring my parents, and all this would be for nothing. But I was unbelievably cold, frightened, and a little lost. I reluctantly agreed and headed inside.

22

THE DOLAN ESTATE

J ust across the threshold and I could already smell exotic and wonderful fragrances of something cooking in the kitchen. Just the reception alone was bigger than our entire living room. It looked more like a hotel. I couldn't even fathom the number of rooms.

'Please leave your shoes here,' she instructed.

We passed by the living room, which was lit by a crackling fire.

My hair was violently tussled. Out from the doorway jumped three perfectly identical boys who wrestled me to the ground. I let out a meek yelp as I collapsed to the floor.

'Who's this?' they said in unison.

They all had straggly brown hair and cheeky blue eyes that just screamed *We're trouble.*

Bree snapped at them furiously. 'He's my friend, you idiots!'

'We know. If he wasn't, he wouldn't be alive to see us coming.'

They pulled me to my feet. I laughed it off. 'Ha. Good one.'

'Have fun!' they said and bounced out of the room, chasing each other up the stairs.

'They seem ... friendly,' I said, adjusting my collar.

Bree rolled her eyes. 'You have no idea.'

She took me up to the kitchen, which was on the second floor of their never-ending mansion. It was incredible. The counters were marble topped, and pots and pans hung from steel hooks. The floor was tiled black and white. They had a maid, of course, who was preparing stew in some sort of giant cauldron on top of the stove.

In the corner was a pet chameleon, which sized me up with its beady eye as I passed. Bree's mum came in through the door and didn't notice me at first. I seized up. She was striding around as if on a mission. 'Mum, have you met Will?' Bree asked.

She continued to inspect the kitchen, testing the stew with her finger. 'No, darling, I—Oh.'

She sauntered right over to me and extended her hand. 'How nice to finally meet you, Will.'

I shook her hand firmly.

'He was in the Space Explorers musical, remember?'

She placed a hand over her mouth. 'Oh dear. I mean ... Oh, yes!'

My nerves started acting up again. It wasn't exactly the memory I wished to be remembered for.

'Well, I thought you were very funny.'

That's what I was aiming for, I guess. 'Thank you, Mrs Dolan.'

She smiled. 'Oh, actually, it's just Ms.'

Bree scratched the nape of her neck.

'Oh, OK, thank you, Ms Dolan,' I said.

She wandered over to the counter and poured from a

pot of tea. 'Here, this'll warm you up,' she said, handing me an oversized mug.

~

BREE'S ROOM wasn't any less impressive. The walls were lined with luxurious paintings, and she had a four-poster bed for starters.

There was a huge wooden dollhouse in the corner. It was blanketed in light that was pouring through the window. I stood like a statue, not knowing where to sit. I hadn't been in a house this classy before. Bree noticed and beckoned me to sit on the carpet.

'I don't play with the dollhouse. Not sure why I have it.'

The interior had such intricate detail, every room lined with hand-carved detailing.

'It's cool if you play with it,' I said.

She shrugged. 'You must think I'm spoiled.'

I blinked heavily and shook my head. 'No, no, I don't. I didn't know your family was so—'

'Rich?'

I half-smiled. 'I was going to say big.'

She adjusted the little dolls and made them walk down the staircase.

'You didn't mention your brothers before,' I said.

'I guess I didn't. We're all a little mad here.'

I laughed. I thought back to the musical. 'How did you do that?'

'Do what?'

'Remember all those lines and act in front of all those people. You're so ... OK with being silly.'

Bree snapped the dollhouse closed and scooched over to me. 'I'll tell you my secret.'

I tilted my head closer to hers.

'I don't care what people think.'

I shook my head in disbelief. 'But all those people. You don't imagine what they're thinking?'

She frowned. 'I don't care what people think. Ever. Neither should you.'

'I can't turn it off. I have this thing ...' I trailed off.

I debated whether to tell her about Phobos. She couldn't literally look inside my head and see them. Nobody could.

'What thing?'

I sighed. 'I can't explain it. But it's something that stops me from being normal.'

She scoffed at the mention of the word. 'Normal? What's so great about being normal?'

I grinned widely, and she beamed right back at me. I took a swig of Ms Dolan's tea. It was like sweet nectar.

I felt a strange, new sensation stirring inside. Somehow, it felt kind of good to let it out. It'd been cooped up inside for such a long time. Phobos didn't even attempt to stop me. In fact, I couldn't hear them at all. Not for the entire time I was there. Bree smiled reassuringly and had that familiar knowing look on her face. She'd had me figured out from the moment she met me.

'Will. All this will pass. I know. I've been bullied since I moved here.'

'You have?'

She nodded. 'I'm the weird computer girl who loves mysteries and running after aliens. Yes, I've been bullied.'

I was stunned. I hadn't stepped back and thought about my friends' feelings. I didn't even consider them. It was a humbling slap across the face.

'Tony loves you. You must know that, right?'

I winced. It stung to hear his name again. 'I ... I guess. He has a funny way of showing it.'

She grimaced hard. 'I have three brothers. The eldest, Daniel, once hid my chameleon in a cupboard for three days. When I found him, he blamed it on my younger brother, Elliot. I got in such a big fight with Elliot. I said I'd never trust him again.'

'Who told you the truth?' I asked.

'The maid. She saw Daniel do it. Elliot didn't ever snitch on him. And Daniel was too scared to admit it.'

I must have had a dumbfounded look on my face. That didn't make sense to me. 'So, you still hate him?'

She shook her head. 'No. I love my brothers. I forgot about it. After a while.'

The bedroom door creaked open, and Bree's mum poked her head round the corner. 'Sorry to interrupt. Tea is ready.'

I put down my mug and grabbed my backpack.

She stopped me with a gentle touch on the shoulder. 'Would you like to stay for tea?' she asked.

I stopped to ponder. Usually, I would've headed straight out the door, having had my fill of human interaction for the day. But this time felt different. I wanted to stay. They had brought me into their home, offered food, and treated me nicely. The least I could do was make an effort. I couldn't keep disappearing.

'Yes, please.'

'OK, I'll ring your mum and let her know you're here.'

Sitting around that table filled to the brim with a delicious, mouth-watering spread of food was heavenly. I felt small in my chair, with strangers surrounding me. But it wasn't like before. I felt welcomed. They didn't judge me for who I was. Bree was my friend. She truly was. Maybe all you need is one special person who will be there for you through thick and thin. Some people don't even get that.

I thanked Bree's family and returned home later that evening.

23

AN UNEXPECTED PLAN

I opened the door to an unwelcoming, stern-faced Mum. She had clearly given an earful to Dad already as he was slouched on the sofa, head buried behind his newspaper. She threatened to never leave the house again in case I decided to have another walkabout.

I collapsed into my bed with a warm belly full of delicious food. It didn't matter I was in trouble. The future looked a little brighter. Yet, I was still reminded of what I'd miss.

I closed my eyes, and every time, I witnessed images of the winter dance flickering across my eyelids. I saw students laughing heartily, drinking fizzy drinks, pulling sick moves on the dance floor. I was being tortured simply by trying to sleep. Was this the handy work of Phobos? Had they returned? Had they gone from saying horrible words to projecting pictures directly into my brain?

TAP! TAP! TAP!

I jumped up at the abrupt knocking at the door.

'Y-yeah?'

Dad entered the room, ushering me to sit down. It was

past nine p.m., my usual bedtime, so I wondered what could have been so urgent.

'Sorry to wake you, lad,' he said, sitting beside me.

'It's OK. I couldn't sleep.'

He pinched my cheek. 'You've had quite a year.' He sighed.

A heavy lump appeared in my throat, so I kept silent, not to let the tears win.

'I know that dance is tomorrow. I know how badly you wanted to go.'

I pulled the sheets over my head, covering myself completely. I didn't want to cry in front of him.

'Mrs Collings is right. There must be consequences.' He stopped and rubbed his forehead. I didn't exactly wish to relive that conversation again.

'But …'

My ears pricked up. *There's a but?*

'If you don't go, you'll be miserable all bloody year.' His stern face steadily grew into a smile. I had to ask him to repeat himself just in case I misunderstood.

'H-how? Mrs Collings … she would see me there.'

He raised his hand to shut me up. 'You don't need to worry about that.'

'And mum?'

'I'll convince her. Don't you worry. I'll use the ol' dad charm.'

I flew out of bed and hugged him in a vice-like grip. This must have caught him off-guard because he nearly lost his balance. He patted my back gently.

It's not often me and Dad would hug like this. It was a rare occasion. But it made it all the more special when we did.

'But …'

Oh no, another but.

'You're grounded for a week after. No going out. Extra homework.'

Little did Dad know that staying indoors was my bread and butter. I stuck out my hand. 'Deal!'

24

DODGE THIS

I t was the day before the winter dance. You know the saying, time flies when you're having fun? Well, it wasn't fun, and time was standing still. When you're so incredibly excited about something, the wait to get there seems endless. But when it happens, it seems to be over in the blink of an eye.

I drummed my fingers on the desk. I gazed out the window and imagined what the dance might look like. I planned to dress in the highest of fashion. Maybe I'd wear sunglasses, or would that be too much? I was overthinking it.

'Hello. Are you home?' inquired Ms Trigger.

'Yes, Ms Trigger,' I said.

She pointed to the whiteboard and asked, 'So, Will, do you think Mr Toad changed by the end of the book?'

'Yes, Ms.'

'And why do you think that?'

I took a hard stare at the book cover. 'He changed because he had friends, and they helped him.'

She hesitated for a moment, then waved her marker at me. 'Right. That's good!'

I noticed Tony, who glanced in my direction, but only for a second or two.

I raised a smile. He flashed me a half smile and turned away. That was some sign of progress, I supposed.

∼

LATER THAT DAY was the final PE class of the year, thankfully. We were gearing up in the changing rooms when the football boys passed behind me. Nick was by the lockers. He whispered something in Alex's ear.

Tony appeared beside me, tying his laces nonchalantly. I tried to gain his attention. I yawned loudly, stretching my arms in a cartoonish way. He ignored it. Mr Owens, our PE teacher, stood in the doorway. He took up the entire frame with his unbelievably wide shoulders.

'Attention, everyone,' he commanded in his ground-shattering voice. 'On account of the rain, rugby practice is cancelled.'

The entire room erupted in whoops and cheers. We all knew what that meant. My entire body sank to sub-zero temperatures. *DODGEBALL!*

My legs trembled, and my palms were sweating. I was the last to be picked. I was always the last. Our team of six consisted of unfit, non-sporty students. I'm not trying to be mean or cruel—I was one of them. I knew full well I wasn't equipped to play this game.

Bree was on my team. Tony was on the opposite team. All the players on his side were huge, brutish boys who played as if their lives depended on it.

I kept my eye on Alex, who was just waiting for any

excuse to hurl that ball into my face and out the other side. I looked up through the skylight of the sports hall and pleaded, *Please let me survive this day.*

The whistle sounded. I ran forwards to pick up the ball but was outrun by Nick, who grabbed it from my grasping fingertips. I stumbled backwards to get away as quickly as possible. He threw the ball at some poor unsuspecting kid, knocking the glasses right off his face. Mr Owens pipped the whistle.

'OUT! Six–Five.'

Bree scooped up the ball and targeted Nick. She threw it hard. But Nick caught it with ease, causing her to crash out.

'OUT! Six–Four.'

After an exhausting battle and many brutal takedowns, it was down to me vs Nick and Tony. I had practically backed myself into a corner by this point. How I had managed to survive that long, I had no idea. Bree and Charlene watched in horror from the sidelines. They didn't know who to cheer for.

'Two–One.'

I knew it was game over, but I wasn't ready to admit defeat. So, I regained my balance steadily and planted my feet firmly on the ground.

But I didn't get a chance to breathe. Nick wound up his arm and belted the ball at me full speed. Before I could even react, it struck me in the chest so hard I doubled over. The wind was forced out of my lungs. He screamed victory and pumped the air. His teammates gave each other self-congratulatory high-fives.

Mr Owens blew the whistle again. 'Foul!'

In a moment of glee—and desperation to get me out—it appeared as though Nick forgot you cannot hit someone above their waist. He was out.

'One–One.'

The oxygen levels hadn't yet returned, but I righted myself to face Tony.

We both stared at each other for a moment. I wished he had a change of heart. I wished he'd turned around and lobbed that ball right into Nick's stupid face. But he didn't.

'On my whistle,' Mr Owens said.

I wiped my sweaty hands on my soaking-wet PE shirt.

The whistle blew.

I quickly grabbed the ball nearest to me. So did Tony. We both jittered about, threatening to throw the ball at any moment. The football boys were yelling, trying to distract me. Mr Owens did nothing to stop them.

We both wound up our arms and launched the balls at catastrophic speeds. They collided with each other mid-air and bounced back towards us. My ball struck my knee. Tony's ball hit his thigh. Mr Owens ended the game right there.

'TIE!'

Everyone went silent. It was a disappointing finish, for sure. But, we tied, which is a better outcome than I could have imagined.

Bree congratulated me. Charlene looked worried.

'What's wrong?' I asked Charlene. 'Better than nothing.'

'No, it's not that,' she said.

'Huh? What do you—'

'Char. Charlene. Over here.' She was quickly summoned over by Nick, as though she was his pet.

'I'm sorry,' she said, then left to join them.

I wondered what had gotten into Charlene, and as I headed to the changing rooms, a strong breeze wafted around my legs.

Huh? Did it just get colder in here? I thought.

I kept on walking, but my feet were getting tangled in something.

A wave of laughter rose. I saw a blur of faces and fingers pointing at me. I looked down.

My shorts were around my ankles. The chilling wind lapped against my bony legs. Goosebumps grew all over. It was humiliating. All the students, the teachers, everyone saw. They pointed and laughed as though I was a clown or something made especially for their entertainment. I fumbled around and quickly pulled them up again, but the silky material kept slipping down. My underpants were on show to the entire school. Then I saw Alex with a giant grin stuck on his big, dumb face. Beside him, Nick was smugly enjoying my misfortune. We all knew who the ringleader was here.

Without hesitation, Tony marched up to Alex and shoved him. This was unexpected for Alex, who lost his footing, tumbling over.

'You think you're funny?' Tony yelled at the top of his lungs.

Nick gestured to Alex not to get up. Instead, he faced Tony himself.

'What are you gonna do? Get your weird friend to make me disappear too?' Nick said.

Tony raised his fists, and Nick just stared back, daring him to strike first. Their foreheads were practically touching.

'I know you did something to them. Thomas and Dave. You are so dead.'

Please, stop, I thought. It was getting too intense, and things were bad enough as they were. I wanted to shrink down and crawl in between the floorboards. Then nobody would know I was there.

'You touch him, and I'll make sure you never play sports again!' Bree barged into the fight, shoving Nick away. But it only made Nick's mad grin spread even wider.

Please. Please. STOP.

'Hey, stop!' Mr Owens rushed over and quashed the situation. He pulled the boys apart with an effortless tug. 'You. Detention.'

He only focused on Tony, which made us all furious.

'But, sir ...' Bree said.

Mr Owens's eyes narrowed on her.

'But nothing. Detention for you, Ms Dolan.'

Bree looked paler than a ghost. Detention was a word she'd never heard before.

'You ... can't ...' I said.

'Fine. All three of you. Detention. Tonight.'

Nothing surprised me anymore. Those responsible never get the punishment they deserve.

∼

IN THE CHANGING room I made sure to get dressed in the bathroom, with the stall door locked. I quietly sobbed to myself, trying to suck up any tears that fell. It felt like I wasn't a 'real man' because I dared to cry. Everyone else got pantsed all the time, and they laughed it off. I felt so weak.

Phobos followed me inside the stall. *'Classic. Why don't you use that shovel to dig yourself a little deeper? Ooo, even better, why don't you simply bury yourself completely?'*

Bury? I thought. Then came a discovery. A eureka moment.

I knew where it was. Our little friend.

TAP TAP TAP

There was a knock at the door. 'P-please go away,' I cried.

'It's Tony. Open the door, mate.'

I cleared my throat and gathered enough energy to speak. 'Oh, hi.'

It was quiet for a moment. You would only be able to make out the sound of tears splashing on the floor.

'It's not right. They can't get away with this,' he said.

I could hear the anger seeping out of him. I wiped my eyes.

'Leave it.'

'No. I don't want to leave it. Not this time. This has to stop.'

He was right. This had to end. I tried ignoring it before, but they weren't going to stop.

Click!

I opened the door. Tony's face was almost purple. He was breathing heavily.

I reached out and laid my hand on his shoulder. 'We will beat them. I think I know how.'

He relaxed his shoulders, and his breathing shallowed.

'I'm sorry,' I said. I was surprised the words escaped my mouth.

'Don't be. I'm sorrier.' He coughed to cover up his quivering voice. 'You idiot.'

We both laughed.

He pulled me in for a hug. It felt good to regain a friend, even whilst having the life squeezed out of me. We were in this together now.

'What's the plan?' he asked.

'First, we're going to break out of detention,' I replied.

25

DETENTION

In the classroom, everyone started to pack up, readying themselves for home. Everyone except me. A noticeable buzz of excitement pulsated through the room. I watched every second tick away on that clock. The guilt overcame me. It was truly terrible to be a new member of the 'naughty kids' group. I had hoped to pass through primary school with a clean record, but now I'd joined the ranks of hooligans and criminals.

I wondered if this would affect my ability to get a job in the future. Would I have a big stain on my report card that read HAD DETENTION IN YEAR 6. DO NOT EMPLOY.

BRRRR!

The bell sounded. Nobody said goodbye to me as they rushed towards the exit like the building was on fire. I ducked away from swinging backpacks and tumbling chairs. Just like that, the classroom was deserted.

Mrs Collings sat undisturbed behind her desk, watching me like a hawk. The tedious ticking of the clock echoed around the still room.

SMASH!

The sound of breaking glass came from another room. Mrs Collings snapped her head to the source of the commotion; the legs of her chair screeched loudly as she got up. 'Wait here. I'll be back shortly.'

I plucked up the courage to speak up before she could leave. 'Ex ... Excuse me, Mrs Collings. Where are my friends?'

She chuckled softly. 'Well, it wouldn't be much of a detention if you were allowed to sit with your friends.'

With that bombshell, she left.

No, no, no, I cried.

I leant backwards and peered out the door. The classrooms had open walls where the doors should be. I could see down the corridor. The IT suite was in the middle of the building, so the corridors were kind of like a big square connecting all the classrooms together.

The staffroom door swung open and after the first swing, I spotted Mrs Collings inside, standing around swigging tea as she spoke on the phone.

'May as well give up now.' Phobos said. Without Tony and Bree, I wouldn't possibly be able to pull this off. I slumped onto the table, feeling as though handcuffs bound my wrists.

'Pssst.'

What was that? A mouse?

'Will!' someone furiously whispered.

I turned around. Bree poked her head out from the corridor. I almost fell out of my chair.

'What are you doing?' I asked.

'Regretting my life choices,' she grumbled.

She crept in and untied the shackles from my wrists.

'Right. Now what's the plan?'

'I'll explain on the way. Let's go.' I surprised myself at how awesome I sounded.

We kept our heads down as we scurried into the corridor. Another teacher swung open the staffroom door, this time wide enough to see further inside. There he was. Tony was sitting on the sofa, head in his hands.

'Why is he in the staffroom?' she asked.

I laughed knowingly. I knew exactly what he was doing. 'He's buying us some time.'

Just before the doors swung closed again, Tony spotted us and gave a cheeky wink.

This time Mrs Collings exited the staffroom and swiftly made her way towards our classroom. Time stood still for a moment. She was going to catch us.

'Go. There,' Bree bumbled as we shot into the IT suite and under a computer desk. We watched through the glass as Mrs Collings stomped her way down the corridor.

'She's going to see I'm not there!' I panicked.

Bree looked equally helpless. 'What can I do?'

'You're the smart one.'

She forgot the situation for a second and blushed. 'Really?'

'Yes!'

Bree looked elated. She had noticed something in the corner. Without a moment's hesitation, she ran up and grabbed the PA microphone, hitting the button.

'Mrs Collings! We need you in Room 203.' Her voice echoed around the whole building.

Mrs Collings stopped in her tracks and looked around, puzzled. It certainly sounded like a little kid had spoken, but Bree sounded confident enough for it to work. She walked back around to Room 203, which was far away from us.

We both shuffled forwards, out the opposite side of the

IT room and through the front exit. It felt like freedom—we could taste it. Just as we approached the final corridor, the glowing green exit sign just metres away, Mr Strange, the headmaster, strolled around the corner. He was a huge man with monstrous shoulders, bulging eyes, and an unmoving, unshakeable grimace permanently etched upon his face.

He strode towards us with gigantic steps, each one hitting the ground with a mighty *THUD*.

We froze in place. I could hear Bree chanting under her breath. She must have been praying; not a bad idea. As Mr Strange approached, I felt as though I should say something, but I couldn't move my quivering lips.

'Goodnight,' he said as he passed right by us.

We couldn't believe it. We laughed, as you do when faced with a life-threatening situation, then waltzed right out the exit.

26

CONTACT

I t was getting late, and the sky was darkening into a deep shade of blue. There was no security on the school grounds, luckily for us. I figured we didn't have long before Mrs Collings would return, so we had to act fast.

Me and Bree tiptoed around the school building, keeping tight against the wall. We were careful not to disturb the late-working teachers still inside. We crouched under each window we passed, each illuminated with orange light splashing out onto the pathway.

'*Now* can you tell me what's going on?' Bree asked.

'We're going to the amphitheatre.' I said. 'If I'm right, then the answer has been under our feet the whole time.'

'What if you're wrong? What if we get caught?'

'Take the adventure, heed the call,' I replied.

She looked impressed. 'You *can* learn.'

We approached the amphitheatre. There were no floodlights, lampposts, anything. The area was completely devoid of light. We stumbled over the harsh grassy bank and kept walking until the sound of crunching gravel came from under our shoes. 'We're here,' I said.

'Will, I'm not sure—'

'Shhh,' I said, holding my hand up to her face.

She batted it away, disgusted. 'Don't tell me to shh!'

'Sorry, sorry. Please, just listen.'

I pressed my ear to the cold ground. As I got closer, that familiar sound came rushing back. I jumped up and down with giddiness.

'That sound. I knew I'd heard it before. Of course, it's under the amphitheatre!' I exclaimed. 'It's circular. The perfect hiding spot.'

She crossed her arms tightly. 'If it's the UFO ... how do you know it'll be friendly this time?'

'It could have taken us. Easily. But it didn't. It only takes bad people,' I said. 'It's here to help us.'

'But how would it know who is bad or not?' she asked. It was a good question.

'I saw the burn marks. The farmer was hurting it. Thomas and Dave? Bullies.'

I suspected Bree wasn't convinced, but I didn't care. I stamped hard on the stony ground. No response. I jumped up and down with both feet, slamming the ground.

With no students around, everything sounded much clearer. It was so serene. The faint noise of the whirring engine began growing into a much harsher scream of moving parts. The ground vibrated, slowly at first, but then became much more intense. My whole body shook so hard that my brain felt like it was bouncing around in my skull.

Then, it settled down. It didn't stop; it just stayed at a consistent level.

WHUM!

A striking flash of green ran through the ground like a ripple through water.

'It's here. It's actually here!' I laughed.

Bree pulled out her notebook and flipped to the pages with all the dots and dashes.

'S-should we start?' she asked, the fear returning to her voice.

I gave her a thumbs-up.

I cleared my throat. 'Hello,' I said.

No reply.

'M-maybe it can't hear you?' she said.

'HELLO!' I hollered.

Four short bursts of green happened in quick succession, followed by a longer one.

.... . .-.. .-.. ---

I couldn't take in all the information at once, but Bree could. She was following each flash closely, matching them with the correct letters. The UFO released its last discharge, and night returned.

'Well, what did it say?' I asked.

She held up her notepad in disbelief. Her hand was shaking. 'It said hello. It … It understands us.'

I rubbed my hands together gleefully. My mind raced wildly; anything was possible now.

'W-what should we say next?'

I handed her a scrunched-up paper note. I had jotted down some ideas. Bree studied and read my poor handwriting the best she could. When she realised what I had written and wanted to ask the alien, her face turned an even paler shade of white.

'Will, I can't … I can't believe—why would you ask this?'

My giddy excitement was crushed. When you have an idea, it sounds great in your head, but when a fresh pair of eyes sees it and tells you it's a bad idea, your world comes crashing down.

'I thought y-you'd like it. It's for all of us, right?'

'No. I think it's for you,' she said.

The blood drained from my face. It was hard to imagine Bree going against me.

'I'm so sorry about what happened, but this isn't going to help. I can't be a part of it.'

'But... I thought—'

'I'm going back inside before they notice I've gone. I think you should too.'

I watched on helplessly as she walked away.

Without my translator, I needed to improvise. I thought of a genius solution. I would ask the alien simple yes or no questions.

'Hi, again. Don't worry about my friend. I need to ask you something. Can you flash once for yes and twice for no?'

The light flashed.

'Good. Good. There is a dance tomorrow. It's really important. Can you help me?'

The light flashed again.

I took a moment. I considered Bree's refusal and how she'd always been right in the past. But the football boys needed to be stopped. For good.

I sighed and looked at the creased note, took a deep breath, and said, 'You probably don't know what people are like. Not yet. They're not all like my friends. Some are mean, like, really mean. We call them bullies. They hurt us for fun. Sometimes, I wish I could fight back, but I can't even talk normally. So, I need your help. Can you take away the bullies? Somewhere far away?'

The air was quiet. Not a peep from the buried machine. Perhaps it needed some time to consider. After all, it was an intelligent creature. Giving up its hiding spot now would be foolish.

I felt stupid for asking, so I turned my back and began walking away. Then, a pulse of green light. Just one.

A wicked smile crept across my face.

27

THE WINTER DANCE

I t was finally time. The winter dance was here.

My wardrobe was a collection of bad fashion choices. As much as I admired my mum, she had awful taste in clothes. But there was a sizzling-hot shirt that I'd been saving for such an occasion. I grabbed it off the hanger. I slipped on my denim jeans and fastened the belt extra tight.

Downstairs, my dad was enacting the first stage of the plan. He'd rung Mrs Collings to apologise for my behaviour and invited her out for dinner. Mum was not pleased. She didn't want to spend an evening with someone she'd described as "the Wicked Witch." I knew these favours would come only once in a blue moon, so I thanked them over and over again until they asked me to stop.

I sauntered downstairs feeling confident, decked out in my outfit. I wore a black shirt with flames lapping at the bottom and a red dragon flying across the chest. Tonight was going to be different. *Not even Phobos can stop me,* I thought.

'We'll see about that,' they replied.

James whistled as I jumped off the final step. Dad had to turn away, stifling his laughter. Mum clapped her hands together and beamed. 'Look at you. Isn't that nice?' She nudged Dad.

He turned around and dropped his smile. 'Oh, yes, you're going to break some hearts tonight,' he said.

I could always count on Dad to be sarcastic.

We headed out to the car. James begged us not to go to the dance. He struggled and fought against us as we dragged him into the car.

'You want us to hire a babysitter?' Mum threatened.

James huffed. 'No.'

'OK, well, you're going with your brother.'

He sulked the rest of the way there.

We were only a few streets away from school. I could hear the distant sound of muffled music, and colourful lights dancing in the sky. My stomach turned queasy. Maybe I wasn't as confident as I first thought. It's great in theory, but being there for real was when doubt started kicking in.

Then I had another idea.

'Dad, can we pop over to Tony's quickly?'

He grunted in an annoyed way but agreed to my wishes. We turned around.

KNOCK, KNOCK!

The door swung open. I was greeted by a rough, haggard middle-aged man. He had a slice of pizza hanging out of his mouth. The sauce was dripping onto his belly.

'Hi, Mr Hitch. Is Tony here?'

He hung on to the door as he turned and yelled up the stairs. 'TONY! DOOR!'

Tony came rushing out. 'Hey ... Oh. Will? You're not going to the dance?'

I rubbed my hands together. 'Oh, I'm going. And you're coming with me.'

Without questioning anything, he assembled an outfit, grabbed his boots, and got into the car in under a minute.

～

AS WE PULLED alongside the school, I felt that sickness rising again. This was the end of an era. Who knew what tonight, and the future, may hold?

As I pulled the car door handle, Dad leant over. 'Have fun, boys, but not too much fun.'

We agreed and headed out.

'And look after your brother!' Mum shouted through the open window.

Off they drove to enact the second stage of the plan. All I could hope was they'd keep Mrs Collings distracted long enough.

So, with James in tow, we'd finally arrived. At the threshold of the school hall, the doorway was lined with a bouquet of blue balloons and students were lining up to go in. Everyone looked so different without their school uniforms; I was underdressed. A lot of boys wore smart dress shirts, properly tucked into their trousers. The girls wore a dazzling array of dresses. I wiped my forehead.

'Hot in here,' I said.

Tony patted my back, which was already growing patches of sweat. 'We were funny, right?' He chuckled.

'Wh-what? When?' I asked.

'The musical.'

'Oh, hah, yeah. They did laugh a lot.'

'They loved it!' He laughed even harder.

The thumping music grew louder as we edged closer to the hall.

'It was going well until you jumped on me and broke the set.'

Tony blushed and hid his face. 'Right ... did I hurt you?' he asked delicately.

I smiled. 'Nah. I'm tough.'

James looked increasingly confused at our conversation. 'What are you talking about?'

'Nothing. Maybe Mum and Dad will show you the video one day,' I said.

The queue began to dwindle. We were almost in. I could smell the buffet.

∽

INSIDE THE HALL was a feast for the eyes. The DJ was set up, playing *the* hottest tunes. Streams of confetti and crepe paper were draped across the walls. The buffet stretched as far as the eye could see. There was an enormous punch bowl as the centrepiece. It oozed elegance. We stood at the back of the hall, observing everyone else.

James spotted his friend from Year 3 but pretended not to see him. He waved James over.

'Isn't that your friend?' I asked.

'Tristan,' he said.

Tristan stomped his foot and commanded him to come over.

James obeyed and wandered over to him without saying a word.

'Stay where I can see you!' I demanded.

His shoulders were deflated, and his head hung like a

wilted flower. I had a feeling perhaps this wasn't exactly a 'friend'. I'd have to keep a close eye on them.

All eyes seemed to divert to the entrance as Bree entered the hall. I had to look twice; she looked so different. She wore a sparkly blue gown, and her hair was all curly and puffy. She looked like a fairy-tale princess. We waved frantically at her, and she came over.

'Wow.' Tony gasped.

She giggled. 'Don't be jealous because I made an effort.'

'You look really nice, Bree, honestly,' I said.

'Thank you. I like your shirt?' she said unconvincingly.

The next to enter were the football boys, dressed sharply in matching black-and-white outfits. Nick was leading the pack. He even wore sunglasses indoors, which was ridiculous, but a fashion choice only he could pull off. Everyone stopped and stared. Even the DJ stopped playing for a second to witness their coolness.

'So, are you going to tell me how you're here right now?' Bree asked.

'Huh?'

'You were banned from the dance.'

'Does it matter?' I replied.

'No, I guess not. And what about our 'friend'? Did you ask them to ... you know?'

'Maybe ...'

Bree's face turned sour. It was the same look a disappointed mother might give you. But I didn't care. The plan was going to happen at some point that night. I just didn't know when exactly.

As we were locked in a match of 'who could look the angriest', a gust of wind blew in, and a luminous white figure glided into the hall. The heavens seemed to have opened. It was Charlene. Somehow, she'd grown even more angelic. She walked over to Nick, like a robot following orders, and linked arms with him. He made sure everyone in the hall saw them.

The tangible anger was radiating from Tony's body. I patted his back to calm him down.

Alex shot a look in our direction. He winked at Tony. I had to physically restrain him from starting a fight.

'They're not going to stop us from having a great night,' Bree said, throwing back a shot of pineapple juice.

'Don't worry, they definitely won't,' Phobos said.

'I'll get us drinks!' Bree went over to the punch bowl.

I couldn't help but notice the sad puppy-dog face Tony was pulling. He stood in the shadows, watching Charlene and the football boys talking and dancing under the bright disco lights.

'You know, I don't think it's worth fighting over,' I said to him.

He wiped his snotty nose and sniffed. 'What isn't?'

'Girls.'

He snorted. 'Yeah, I guess not.'

Tony shuffled nervously on the spot. He seemed anxious to ask me something. 'Do you think, if the deal was still happening, you would dance with her?'

'Yeah. I think so.'

He looked down at his shoes.

'But it didn't happen. And I got my best friend back. I think that's better.'

He swallowed me up in a massive hug. 'Thank you.'

Bree came over with our drinks. 'I see you boys made up.'

'Can I have the one with more concentrate?' Tony asked.

'Sure.' She handed him the cup.

'I need a strong drink.'

'Oh.'

Tony chugged his pineapple juice, wiped his lips, and cracked his knuckles. His mood had certainly improved. He turned to Bree with his eyes twinkling bright. 'Do you wanna dance?'

She looked at me with utter shock. I was just as surprised.

'Uh ... I don't know. I'm a pretty bad dancer. It's embarrassing,' she said.

I shot Bree a look of bewilderment. 'I thought you didn't care what people think?'

She was taken aback. I had used her own words against her. 'Touché,' she said.

Tony took her hand and whisked her onto the dance floor amid the other students. I couldn't help grin like an idiot, seeing my two best friends having the time of their lives. Then I felt a twinge of sadness. This might be the last time we got to do this together.

The party was now in full swing. The popular kids were bunched up together like a deadly hornet's nest. I stayed far away from the dance floor with all the outcasts who barely had the confidence to go to the dance in the first place.

I kept my eye firmly on the football boys, who seemed to be planning something. But something even more alarming caught my eye.

Through a gap in the crowd, I saw James with his 'friend' Tristan. He had James in a headlock.

I raced over to them. I had to be delicate—it was only a little kid, after all, and I was bigger.

Tony saw the fuss and rushed over to us. 'Just say the word, and I'll hit the twerp ...'

I stopped him. I didn't think sending a Year 3 to hospital was the best idea.

'Oi. L-leave him alone,' I bellowed at Tristan.

He released James from his headlock. He stumbled backwards, face like a beetroot.

Tristan tussled his hair. 'We're just having fun, aren't we, James?'

James looked down and mumbled, rubbing his sore neck.

Then Tristan tried to grab his arm, but James pulled away. He tried again, this time forcefully, and yanked him closer.

James pulled up his weary head for the first time. He looked the bully squarely in the eyes and smiled. I'd never seen him look so confident. It was a little frightening.

In a flash, he planted a fist right into Tristan's nose. He stumbled and landed hard onto his backside.

Tony and I were left stunned and speechless. James flicked his wrist in pain.

'Well done, mate!' Tony fist-bumped him on his opposite hand.

'Thanks,' James said, raising a smile.

~

THE DJ SCRATCHED the record to a halt and tapped his microphone. Everyone gathered around him. 'Ladies and gentlemen, take your places for the "Swing Hop Dance".'

Bree came bounding up and tried pulling me onto the dance floor. I resisted, keeping my feet firmly planted to the sticky floor. As anyone with two left feet knows, looking cool while dancing is impossible. I thought I'd sink to the bottom of the social barrel.

'Bree, I don't know ...'

But it was too late. I was already lined up in a row with a

group of excitable students. I anticipated the beat drop. But something was ... off. Any minuscule amount of sound was sucked out of the room to create a noiseless vacuum. My arms were locked by my side, and my legs were cemented to the floor. I felt their presence stronger than ever before.

Phobos.

'You thought it was that easy?' Their words snaked around my head. *'You thought I was gone? I own you. You're about to become the most embarrassing moron in here.'*

I tried to wiggle my way out, but every muscle in my body was constricted.

The needle dropped, and the bass shook the school's foundations. Everyone joined in and followed along to the DJ's instructions. 'Swing to the left,' he said.

A couple of girls bumped into me and tripped over. I stayed glued to my position.

'Sorry,' I said. But the words barely trickled out of my mouth.

Other students had started to notice my lamppost-like pose. They whispered to each other.

'Why did he come here?'

'He's so awkward,' they said.

My neck resisted the turn, but I could manage to move it enough to spot Tony breakdancing terribly on the floor and Bree laughing along with him. I felt a warmth starting to grow and sprout in my chest.

'Hop to the right,' the DJ said.

A tingling sensation came back into my lower legs. I could wiggle my toes.

I felt a distant drumming on my shoulder. Bree was twirling her hair, dancing without a care in the world. My feet began to tap.

Then I turned left and caught Charlene's gaze, who

gifted me her trademark smile. My arms broke free like a baby bird taking its first flight. It didn't matter what they thought.

'Everybody, dance!'

It was as if someone replaced my eyes with a fresh pair. The students weren't looking at me at all. They were having fun with their friends. Nobody was talking about me. Phobos fumed and raged, but I didn't care. I broke into a frenzy of dance, my arms flailing like a fish on land. I was unstoppable. Everyone froze and stared at the crazed flame-shirted boy on the dance floor.

The other students pointed and laughed at first but quickly became won over by my pure lack of care. I was in another world. A bunch of students got into a line alongside me and copied my moves. We danced in sync together.

The football boys slapped their knees, howling with laughter. But Benny wasn't joining in. He looked irritated. He went to move, but Alex put a hand firmly on his shoulder. He shook off Alex's grip and joined in our ridiculous dance.

For those three minutes, all fears vanished. I was lost in the music with my friends and strangers alike, all sharing a connection for a moment. The spotlight wasn't for me; it was for all of us.

28

PRIMAL FEAR

B*ANG!*
The hall doors slammed open with such force that the gust of wind blew over several decorations. The music shuddered to a halt.

Bone-chilling wind bathed the room. Through the bright lights and dry ice, I could just make out Mrs Collings glaring at us from the doorway. The red LEDs reflected in her eyes like a fiery volcano ready to erupt. The plan had fallen through. Game over.

'Tony! Will!' she shouted.

I panicked and looked at Tony in search of an escape, who looked equally helpless.

Somehow, the students knew what to do. They swarmed her, jumping up and pulling on her arms.

'Hi, Mrs Collings.'

'Come dance, Mrs Collings!'

She batted them away, but they kept on swarming her like flies.

In the chaos, we didn't waste any time and ran out of the hall. Down the corridor we sprinted full speed.

'Where's Bree?' I asked breathlessly.

'No idea!' he said.

'O-OK. W-where to?'

Tony grabbed my arm. 'This way!'

We veered to the left and out the side exit door.

We were plunged into the unforgiving winter chill. I grabbed my chest out of pure shock from the cold.

'N-now w-what?' I hugged myself to stop shivering.

Tony beckoned me to follow. We edged our way around the corner of the school building. We walked past a classroom window. The shadowy figure of a teacher appeared. We ducked down. We slid our feet along the gravel and kept moving at a snail's pace.

'Next corner, we're nearly there,' Tony whispered.

We had just managed to slip around the corner when I bumped into a large object blocking the way. I bounced off it and fell to the ground. If matters couldn't be made any worse, it was the football boys. Alex and Nick were at the front of the group. Benny was at the back, standing far away from them.

'Nice night,' Nick said joyfully.

Tony pushed me aside and took an attack position.

'Come here,' Nick yelled.

From the back of the group, Charlene and Bree were brought out, kicking and screaming.

Tony raised his fists. 'Don't you touch them!'

Alex restrained the girls as they kicked and snarled.

'What did you do with Thomas and Dave?' Nick asked calmly.

'What on earth are you talking about?' Bree spat.

Alex shook the two girls. 'Shut up and listen!'

Nick waved his hand like a magician. Alex fell silent and stepped back in line.

'Benjamin. Give them to me,' he called over. Benny stepped forward with a pair of scissors in his hand. Nick picked them up and waved them about dangerously.

I went into panic mode. How could he have gotten them? This was it. The key piece of evidence that surely would have us thrown in a prison cell. But anywhere would be better right now than here with these psychos.

'Now, Benjamin, you saw Thomas and Dave with these two, right?' Nick asked.

Benny stayed silent.

'Right?' Nick asked with a hint of desperation in his voice.

Benny kept up his unreadable face.

'Right?!' Nick lost his cool. He swivelled around, aiming the scissors right in his face.

Finally, Benny replied. 'No. I didn't see them.'

Nick crumpled up his face and veered around furiously, stomping his feet like a toddler.

'You're useless. Leave. And you ...' He gestured over to Charlene. 'You were helping them.'

She shook her head wildly.

'N-n-n,' I stuttered.

'No. She didn't do anything!' Tony screamed.

Nick laughed. 'Doesn't matter. I only kept her around because it made you boys hate each other. But now you seem to be buddies again. Enjoy being the only friends you'll ever have.'

He took Charlene by the arm and tossed her at us. I caught her before she smacked the concrete floor.

'You have one chance.' Nick turned to face me. 'You. I saw you go into those woods in the playing field. Did you take them there?'

I stood there silently. A tinge of darkness poked my back.

I suspected it was Phobos, but it wasn't them. I was instead drawn to the piercing black outline of the woods. It was calling to me again.

'We didn't do anything to them!' Bree willingly fought back.

'OK. Chance gone,' Nick concluded. He snapped his fingers.

I came back to reality.

The boys strode towards us. The trees groaned, and the wind whipped the grass, making an intense rustling sound that grew louder and louder.

'Listen,' I uttered.

They didn't. They kept on towards us like mindless zombies.

'Just ... l-listen.'

They encircled us, almost blocking out the light. We were about to become minced meat.

'SHUT UP AND LISTEN!' I screamed.

The sound rang out for miles and echoed back again. I didn't think I could reach that volume. All of us stopped and listened to the rushing air. I could see Nick had heard something; his face twinged. He shook his head as if he rejected it.

'You're right,' I said.

Nick's gaze locked with mine. 'Right about what?'

Tony and Bree shook their heads. Begging me to stay silent. But I didn't acknowledge them.

'I took them. Thomas and Dave. Over there,' I said, pointing at the trees.

'He lies,' Alex said.

Charlene tugged at her restraints. 'No, he's telling the truth. I saw them!' she said.

Now I had Nick's attention.

'Show me,' he said.

Before I could respond, suddenly, the light was snuffed out by a great shadow looming over us all.

Is it the beast?

We turned around sheepishly. Yet again, I had been fooled. There appeared Mrs Collings. She stood defiantly, hands placed on her hips.

'Found you,' she said with a look of devilish delight.

29

CLOSE ENCOUNTERS

She marched in between us and stomped her foot down hard.

'Uh, hi, Mrs Collings,' Alex stumbled, letting his captives go.

'What is all this? What are you doing out here? Can you kids just stay out of trouble for once!'

Mrs Collings glared at us, perhaps wondering who she should punish first. It was like watching a kid in a sweet shop.

If I told her about the football boys, it wouldn't only be me who'd get a lifetime membership in the bullying club, but everyone I cared about. I lowered my gaze to the ground, feeling a faint tremor under my feet. I looked closer. Tiny speckles of stone were vibrating along the floor.

'I understand,' Mrs Collings said.

I lifted my head, startled. I was expecting a raging bull, not this.

She bent down to see me eye to eye. 'You want to see your friends. You're trying to get out more, to be social. I shouldn't restrict that.'

Whatever my parents had said to her, it seemed to have worked.

She closed the gap between us. I backed away, still wondering if it was a trap or not.

'I've been teaching for a long, long time. Sometimes I forget to be kind. Nobody gets better by yelling at them.'

I felt so overwhelmed. More importantly, I felt heard. Tears began forming. Normally, I would be too embarrassed to let anyone see, but I didn't care.

'I'm going to try harder, Miss,' I choked out.

As I blinked the tears away, there was a faint glow of green in my blurred vision.

There was a collective gasp from everyone.

WHUM!

I peeked and was greeted by the sight of Mrs Collings floating and rotating in mid-air. We all instinctively tilted our heads upwards to witness the enormous UFO hovering above. She was caught in the tractor beam.

'Wha-huh?' she babbled as she rose higher and higher towards the blinding light.

She was sucked into the ship, which then shuttered its hatch. The light disappeared.

'*AHHHHH!*' everyone screamed.

I was mortified. This wasn't what we had agreed. The UFO didn't care who or what it sucked up. It did whatever it wanted.

Tony pulled at his hair. 'It's really real!'

The entire school flooded out into the playground to see what all the fuss was about. They were instantly pulled in by the extra-terrestrial light. Every light in the surrounding area blew out and plunged the entire school grounds into terrifying darkness.

With the football boys still gawping at the flying saucer,

this was our chance. Bree kicked with all her might and hit Alex in the shins. He howled, and she took off onto the playing field. Charlene went after her. Before Alex could chase after the girls, Tony jumped on his back and began pummelling him. I took my shot and tried wrenching myself out of Nick's grip, but he held onto me for dear life.

Nick forcefully pulled me towards the woods. I feared what lay waiting in there.

'You're going to show me where they are,' he said.

Only the occasional explosion of green lit up long enough for us to see ahead. He stayed behind me the entire time, nudging and prodding me with the scissors every time I slowed down.

'You're ... sure they're still here?' he asked.

'You'll see.'

He shuddered.

As we approached the edge of the woods, it was impossible to see inside. We both squinted, but apparently eating carrots does not in fact help you see in the dark.

Nick clutched the scissors with his sweaty hand.

'You first.' He grunted. I was forcefully squeezed through the narrow entrance.

I was now surrounded by groaning, creaking trees, swaying in the wind. There was no sign of the beast. Nick grew impatient. 'Well, where are they?'

I aggressively 'shushed' him when suddenly the wind dropped.

It was so quiet you could hear a pin drop on a pillow.

CRUNCH!

The underbrush up ahead began twisting and deforming. The freakishly tall creature appeared right in front of us. I didn't need to see well; the smell alone was overpowering. It took another mighty step forward and bent down until it was eye level with me. I investigated its beady black eyes. There was a slight twinkle in there. I noticed my heartbeat, but it didn't seem to quicken in the slightest. In fact, it didn't seem scary at all, more like a giant dog. As I gazed into its eyes, I saw myself in its reflection. I stretched out my hand. It pulled away at first but then returned. I gently pet its tangled fur.

SLASH!

Nick came striding in and slashed at the beast with the sharp blades of his scissors. 'You ugly thing!' he yelled.

The beast groaned and yanked its paw away.

I grabbed Nick's wrist. 'No! You're upsetting it!'

We both tugged at the scissors.

The beast reared its head, exposing its fearsome tusks, and let out a horrifying *ROAR*.

Nick shook in his shoes. I pulled back on his arm and begged him to run, but he pushed me over. I lost my grip on the scissors and fell to the leaf-ridden ground.

'You work for me, OK? You're going to take me to them.' He lurched at the beast aggressively, threatening to cut it again, which didn't seem to have any effect at all.

It didn't occur to me at the time what was going through his mind. Perhaps he thought he could control the beast.

It grabbed the scissors from Nick's hands, but he didn't let go. Instead, it lifted him into the air, his legs dangling helplessly. They were face-to-face now. Nick stretched his hand towards mine. He reached out as far as he could, almost touching my fingertips.

'Help!' he pleaded.

But the beast snatched him away, raising him even higher.

Then the impossible happened. Some emotion came over me I never thought I'd experience until this very moment. I felt pity for Nick. But there was nothing more I could do. So, I ran.

There was no stopping to look back. I scrambled across the dewy, muddy ground and cleared the woods.

'*AHHHHHH!*'

A bloodcurdling scream cried out into the night. Then, nothing.

As I fought through the long grass, I could make out the playground. All the while, the UFO hung ominously above, floating around the school, sucking up innocent victims at random.

SHUM!

The UFO zoomed over the school building. It picked up Ms Trigger and Mr Strange.

I ran over to Tony. 'What just happened? That was ...'

'Crazy? Yeah,' he said, full of energy.

'Where's Nick?' he asked.

I couldn't even stop to explain.

'Where's Bree?'

He shrugged. Through the panic and pandemonium of the students darting around the playground, we couldn't spot her.

We struggled our way through the crowd of kids, stumbling and bumping into them.

My little brother, James, was standing in the playground, entranced by the destruction. 'You need to get inside!' I yelled at him.

'The giant took them,' he said.

'Huh?'

'The giant man took your friends over there,' he said, pointing at the cluster of chestnut trees on the edges of the field.

I knew only one person that could be described as a 'giant'. Alex must have taken the girls.

'OK, Tony, take care of him, I'll be back.'

Tony grabbed my wrist. 'Nah, mate, I'm coming with you.' He was buzzing with fury.

I pushed him back gently.

I always stood around, letting Tony fight my battles for me. But not this time.

'Look, I know you feel like you need to protect me, but I've got this. It's my mistake to fix.'

He took a few deep gulps of air and relaxed his shoulders. He gave me a nod of acceptance.

The twisted branches of the chestnut trees whipped around in the breeze. I was alone but not afraid. As I approached them, I spotted three silhouettes underneath the farthest tree. Two of them had long hair, the other had stocky, broad shoulders.

'Will! This psycho got us!' Bree cried out.

I gulped as I realised who the other girl was.

'Will? Is that you?'

It was Charlene. As the green light blared again, it lit up Alex's crazy expression. He had both Charlene and Bree held tightly by their hair.

He backed up as I approached.

A twig snapped underneath my shoe.

'Stop!' he yelled. 'Don't come any closer, freak.'

I raised my hands to surrender.

'I don't know how, but you did all this.'

I looked around at the devastation happening around us. Maybe he was right, and I was to blame. I didn't intend to harm anyone, but people got hurt all the same.

His grip intensified. The girls whimpered.

'Please, Alex, they didn't do anything. If you want to punish someone, I'm right here.'

A gust of wind blew harshly against us, and the branches of the tree swayed above. I noticed we were standing directly under a clump of conkers—dangling dangerously over us. They were still in their sharp, spiky shells.

I beckoned for Bree and Charlene to look up. As they did, they knew what to do.

'No,' Alex snapped. 'I'm going to keep these two. You know why?'

I tensed. 'Why?'

A terrifying smile crept across his dumb face. 'Because it'll hurt you more.'

As he laughed, I signalled to the girls. 'Now!'

In an almost perfectly rehearsed move, the girls elbowed Alex in the ribs. Hard. He instantly let go of them and stumbled backwards. His head thumped the tree with a great *THUD*!

With the conkers barely hanging on by a thread, they snapped loose, plummeting towards Alex. The sound of a hundred clinking mini daggers came down on him. We dove out of the way as they fell.

We looked away from the horror; we dared not see the aftermath.

The three of us limped back towards the playground, looking like we'd fought in a great battle. I supposed we had.

Tony was sheltered under a bench with James. We reunited and huddled together. I was just relieved it was finally over.

Nothing could be worse than this, I thought naively.

Just as we thought the coast was clear, the roar of the UFO's engines approached. It aligned itself directly above us. We looked at each other hopelessly. Even if we ran, the tractor beam would gobble us up before we got to cover.

The steel hatch of the UFO opened, and we peered up inside it. This time, there wasn't a green glow but a dazzling array of flashing lights.

'W-what's it doing?' Tony quizzed.

'It's Morse code,' Bree said.

She followed the pattern of the lights:

-.. .. ... .- .--. .--. --- .. -. - . -..

AS THE SHIP completed its sequence, the lights shut off, rendering it almost invisible. The engines spooled up and whirred, which shook the ground. We cowered at the sudden blast of air.

It vanished.

We all faced Bree, looking for answers.

'Well, what did it say?' we asked.

'It said, "Disappointed".'

We all paused for a moment, reflecting on its confusing message. I had a sneaking suspicion it might have been talking to me.

We headed home that night, shaken and cold. One by one, we dropped each other off at our various homes, awaited by worried parents who embraced us warmly.

James and I reached our home at last. Mum was already waiting out on the street; she couldn't help but blubber as she held us.

They tried to extract information about what happened that night but to no avail. We kept our mouths well and truly sealed.

∿

THE NEXT MORNING was met by a media frenzy. Dad returned from the newsagents with the local newspaper in hand. They had already published an article: 'Close Encounters of the Countryside.' Alongside the article was a blurry picture of the UFO, but it was hardly concrete evidence.

'Can I read that after you?' I asked him.

'Sure.' He handed it to me.

I stared in disbelief at the author of the article: Bree Dolan. 'Huh, I guess she really did make it.' I grinned proudly.

I read on. Apparently, Alex was wheeled out of school on a trolley, needles sticking out of him like he'd rolled around in an acupuncture clinic. He wasn't badly hurt, but I doubted he'd be playing conkers anytime soon.

Nick looked as if he had been dragged by his ankles through several pine trees, twigs and leaves sticking out of his poofy hair, but was otherwise fine. All the missing UFO abductees were found ten miles away by an incredibly confused farmer. Oh, and Thomas and Dave were there, too. They were all piled up in a pig pen. They must have smelled like the foulest toilet you've ever come across. But I was glad they were safe in the end.

I had a suspicion our alien ally was still out there somewhere, but maybe not. I think it'd have had enough of humanity after seeing what we're capable of. I would do the same in its position.

30

ENDING

B y the end of Year 6, I felt a great sadness. Despite everything I went through, I couldn't help recounting all the incredible memories I had made. It's funny, I spent most of my time thinking only about the bad. But when I look back, I only remember the good, and the friends that stuck by me.

Tony and I were going to attend secondary school together. I was so relieved. I needed someone familiar to guide me through this next chapter of the unknown. Unfortunately, Bree wasn't coming with us. She would attend some private school on the other side of town. All the rich kids went there. At least she was still close.

We promised to still see each other, and always call if we spotted anything strange or unusual.

I went to visit the secondary school I would be attending: Barnfield. *Nothing could be worse than primary school*, I naively thought. *I'm an adult now*.

As I approached the gates, I remember thinking it looked even more impressive than my imagination could conjure. Seeing it up close, knowing my future was held within those bricked walls. The buildings seemed endless. It must have been at least three times bigger than Barnsmead Park. The sports field seemed fit for the Olympic Games. The cream-coloured buildings, all identical to one another, stacked and multiplied as far as the eye could see.

How will a tiny, helpless kid such as me survive in this concrete jungle? Once entered, how is it even possible to find the exit again?

All these questions and more swirled around my brain like a goldfish in a bowl. I knew one thing was certain: I would have to take Phobos with me.

'I'll always be with you,' Phobos said.

Can I ask you something?

They brewed and boiled with anger. That I would dare talk back.

Why me? Why did you pick me?

Then, they replied with a sinister tone. *'You let me in. Remember that.'*

Phobos wouldn't tell me what they meant by that. I would have to figure it out by myself. If there was some way to get rid of them once and for all, surely this would be the place to do it. After all, I must grow out of it sometime, right?

The End

ABOUT THE AUTHOR

Liam Bellamy is an author who loves the strange and the unknown. He wrote this book based on his own adventures and nightmares from his time at Primary School. You're never alone, not if you have imagination. Follow him for more:

- **Behind the Scenes**
- **Exclusive Content**
- **Deleted Chapters**
- **And more...**

Please consider leaving a review or rating on my Amazon or Goodreads page!

KEEP READING after this page for the **QUIZ** and an exclusive look at CHAPTER 1 from the next book in the 'An Introvert's Journey' series.

instagram.com/liambellamybooks

goodreads.com/liambellamybooks

MULTIPLE-CHOICE QUIZ: TBWFHOR

1. What is the name of Will's hometown?
    A. Fielding
    B. Barnsmead
    C. Dower
    D. Barnfield

2. What do Will, Bree, and Tony call themselves?
    A. The Weirdos
    B. The Freaks
    C. The Mystery
    D. The Chameleons

3. What name does the anagram spell: SHOPBO

_____

4. What does Nick make Will do in the chapter *The Newsagent Debacle?*
    A. Read a comic book
    B. Eat sweets
    C. Sing a song
    D. Steal sweets

5. Which word is the best way to describe Will's personality?

    A. Nervous

    B. Confident

    C. Sad

    D. Boring

6. Who is the first person to be taken by the UFO in the chapter *The Break-in?*

    A. Thomas and Dave

    B. The Farmer

    C. Bree

    D. Will

7. How did Tony help Will win the game of conkers in the chapter *The Rematch?*

    A. He swapped Will's conker with a painted metal ball

    B. He made the conker smell like vinegar

    C. He cheated and let Will go first

    D. He didn't help

8. How does Phobos plan to get rid of the football boys in the chapter *The Garage*?

    A. Scare them away with a giant conker

    B. Get Tony to fight them

    C. Ask them nicely to leave

    D. Ask the alien to take them away

9. What is Will's Dad's plan to keep Mrs. Collings away from the winter dance?

    A. He'll have another parents evening

    B. He'll invite her for dinner

    C. He'll take her shopping

    D. He'll play football with her

10. What is a theme of the book?
    A. Conquering fears
    B. Growing up
    C. Friendship
    D. All of the above!

31

BOOT CAMP

I had finally made it. I was now in secondary school. The place where I'd grow up.

Through the steely gates we marched, in single-line formation. Our footsteps were almost perfectly synchronised. Our bulky backpacks weighed heavily on our shoulders. The classroom windows reflected the dying summer sun back at me. The Year 11s were banging against the windows as we passed them, snarling and growling like animals. We were fresh meat, so to speak, perfect targets for the older students. I quickened my pace to pass them.

I was surrounded by a smattering of unfamiliar faces. Both forward and behind me in the line, I couldn't place where they had come from. They certainly weren't from Barnsmead Park.

I decided to wait to speak, as I hadn't yet thought of something insightful to say. You may have faced these situations before when placed in a new environment. You're all in the same camp, yet words escape you, except the occasional, 'Nice day, isn't it?' or 'Wonder what's for lunch?'

I searched desperately through the line of shuffling

soldiers, praying to catch a glimpse of my best friend. I'd lost him a while back on our trek here.

'Get back in line!' a prefect ordered.

I shuffled back into formation.

'HALT,' another prefect commanded.

We stopped abruptly outside of what looked to be the main school hall. It was rectangular and completely ordinary-looking. The boards of wood that made up the walls were shedding their paint like a molting dog.

'Attention!'

Everyone placed their hands by their side in uniformity. I tried mimicking them; my arms stiffly pointed downwards, unnaturally. I didn't know what we were waiting for. I always needed a plan; I hated the unexpected.

The side door of the school hall creaked open, and out of it appeared a small woman with curled hair, dark green blazer, and impossibly high heels. She confidently strutted across the concrete-laden playground and came to a halt in front of the awaiting recruits. If she wasn't wearing those shoes, I don't think she'd have been visible to anyone beyond the front row. She had sharp features, like a bird of prey. Her eyes were small and piercing, her mouth neither smiling nor frowning. They were presets, like a video game character before you modified them.

The quietness of the playground is what struck me most. No children could be heard playing, not even the sounds of birds in trees. This seemed odd for such a massive place.

We awaited the tiny woman to speak. The surrounding teachers stood patiently with their arms crossed, scouring the recruits with glowering eyes, looking for signs of trouble.

She shuffled forwards slightly, adjusted her belt, which

was strapped tightly around her waist, and produced a fake-sounding cough.

'*Ahem.* Welcome'—the sound of her booming voice startled me. It was bizarre to hear that volume come from such a tiny thing—'Welcome to Barnfield Secondary School. I'm Mrs Fawkes, your headteacher.' She leaned forward as though she was expecting us to clap. She raised her eyebrows in displeasure.

'Hm. Well, now you're here, you'll soon learn this is no stroll in the park.' She started creeping down the middle row, placing each step with great purpose. 'For those who couldn't afford Sheppy's school, this was your only option. Please be reminded we are in direct competition with them. They have better facilities, offer more specialized programmes, quality, curriculum, the list goes on...'

My heart rate elevated as she approached my location. I looked down so as to not initiate any unnecessary eye contact. She stopped just short of me and swivelled to the student ahead. She studied him from head to toe, as if she was sizing him up.

'Hm. I swear these Year 7s get shorter every year,' she observed.

'*Ha. She's one to talk,*' said Phobos.

I nudged myself in the ribs, which wasn't the best decision. *Shhh! Ow.*

My previous attempts to be rid of Phobos had all but proven fruitless. I tried mentally blocking them out by listening to 'The Annoying Frog' on repeat until I almost went deaf. But even that irritating amphibian looping around in my head wasn't enough to shake them off. They would break through the barrier every time, feeding me more cynical thoughts and doubt.

It's early days, I thought. *I've only just joined secondary school; he'll be long gone by the time GCSEs roll around.*

'*Keep telling yourself that,*' they sneered.

'So,' she continued, 'don't cause any fires, don't smoke behind the school shed, and don't start fights you can't finish because you certainly won't be going to Sheppy's when we boot you out the door.' She pulled what I believe was supposed to be a smile and trotted back through the hall door, slamming it shut.

'Roll call!' barked the supervising teacher.

One by one the students answered the register, a tedious task, considering there were over a hundred and fifty of us. For most, this is a mundane task, but not for me. My heart rate jacked up several notches if I was acknowledged even a tiny bit.

They finished calling the 'A's', and my palms started to itch.

'Barnaby?' droned the teacher.

A couple of students behind me could barely stifle their laughter. I didn't understand why. It wasn't funny.

Beads of sweat were forming on the back of my neck.

'H-here,' I squeaked.

'Barnaby?' he repeated. More snickers.

'He-present,' I said at the same volume.

'Absent,' he said, checking the box on the register.

How humiliating. Now the school doesn't even acknowledge I'm here.

Tony spotted me through the crowd. He could recognize my meek, timid voice from anywhere. He gifted me a big thumbs-up. I returned the favour.

In a sea of faces, I wanted only to be reunited with my best friend. I figured I would make new friends at some point, but I wasn't ready, not yet.

For some, being thrown into a pile of new faces is a treat, a sheer delight, as they can converse and begin to make life-long memories. I saw it more like being thrown into the fiery pits of hell. It was torment, torture, turmoil, all the t's you can think of.

The door flung open again, and a new face emerged. She was lanky and had a frizzy beehive of hair sitting on top of her head. She wore half-moon spectacles that reflected the sunlight brightly. Somehow, the atmosphere soothed as she approached the podium; she had a much calmer demeanour than the headteacher.

'Good morning, little prodigies. I'm your deputy head-teacher, Miss Yalden.' She scanned the crowd and smiled proudly. 'You're about to embark on a new journey. You'll make new friends, reach new heights, and connect with the world.' She looked as though tears were about to shoot out at any moment. She continued. 'It's of the utmost importance to me that each and every one of you reaches your full potential. I won't let anyone get in the way of that.'

Some students made fun of her admittedly cheesy speech, but at least she seemed more positive than Mrs Fawkes. I knew I needed that more than anything.

Eventually we reached the point where we'd split into our tutor forms. The forms were named with the tutor's initials, so, for example, teacher Aaron Aaronson's class would be 7AA.

I twiddled my thumbs, anxiously awaiting this moment. *Please be with Tony, please be with Tony*, I chanted under my breath.

'Mr Hutch,' Miss Yates announced. '7DJ.'

Tony flashed me a smile as he briskly went off to join his group. They'd already begun chatting and getting to know each other. They disappeared into the school and somehow it felt final, like the closing of a book.

Maybe it was the effects of her rousing speech, or the sweet summer air, but I refused to give in to negativity. No, I was going to be put into 7DJ and—

'Mr Barnaby. 7SS!' she announced.

My hope was crushed in an instant. It deflated like a sad old balloon.

'What did I tell you?' Phobos said smugly.

They were right. Why should I get my hopes up, only for them to come crashing down to earth again.

I looked over at the awaiting tutor, who looked remarkably similar to Mrs Collings, my old primary school teacher. She had this intense stare that was heightened by down-turned eyebrows that formed a permanent scowl.

She beckoned me over.

I joined the other students in 7SS with my head down and sleeves pulled over my hands. I felt everyone's eyes pressing into me. I hated being the last person called.

On we marched inside the building. It was colder than Barnsmead, and all the colour was sucked out. In fact, the school seemed devoid of any warmth. Gone were the pastels and bright displays of finger paintings and times tables posters. They were replaced with endless red steel lockers and dull white walls. It reminded me of the sterile interior of a hospital.

We finally approached our tutor room in the science section of the school. That wasn't the end of the journey, as the room itself was three floors up. We trekked up the stairs and finally made it to the top. The room was a laboratory; Bunsen burners stood to attention, chemicals lined up on shelves, sinks occupied the spaces where our desks should have been. Before entering the room, just outside, we'd passed a cupboard with a giant yellow *WARNING* sign plastered across it. That was a tempting invitation for any young troublemaker.

'Please find a seat,' our tutor instructed.

Oh God. I sighed. At this point I hadn't uttered a word to anyone. The ground trembled like an earthquake. Everyone around me scrambled to sit down. Some even fought over chairs. They'd already found their partner, or at least were the lucky ones who got to keep their friends from primary school.

The dread returned in an instant. *'Nobody wants to sit with you,'* whispered a seething voice. The floor was suddenly caked in acidic chemicals. It was waist-high. My body began sinking into a messy puddle of goop. I didn't resist. At least I'd be gone without a trace; nobody would have even known I existed in the first place. I—

'There's a free seat here,' said a deep voice.

I stared gormlessly at my shoes. They were still intact—not even a drop of acid scuffed them. Phobos was up to their old tricks.

'Yo,' said the voice again.

I snapped out of it and looked at the boy who offered me a chair. He patted the seat and nodded. I couldn't believe he'd actually noticed me.

I gently pulled the chair out and sat down. Even sitting, the boy was noticeably taller, and bigger, than me, at least by one head. He had curly light brown hair and a smattering of freckles.

He extended his hand. Usually people would ignore me completely, like how a lion might ignore a flea. Insignificant. I wasn't sure what to make of it. Was it a trap? Was there a buzzer on the other side that would give me a small electric shock?

'Conor,' the mysterious boy said. He took my hand by force and slapped it into his. I gave in and shook.

'Conor—I mean Will. You're Conor...' I said awkwardly.

He didn't seem to mind my horrible social cues. At least, I think he didn't, I couldn't tell for sure.

The tutor took her position at the front and observed her fresh recruits. She smacked her lips and clapped her hands together. 'Right. Welcome to 7SS.' Her theatrical voice rang out and carried past the back row. Everyone immediately ceased their conversations and turned all their attention on her.

'I'm Mrs Shaxley. Susan Shaxley, hence, our name, SS. See this?' She rapped the desk with her knuckle. 'This is the chemistry lab. It's also our tutor room. So, first and foremost, do NOT mess with it.' She scowled at the students sitting at the back. She'd already picked out the most likely culprits. The group of boys nudged each other and laughed.

'DO NOT touch any chemicals, beakers, Bunsen burners, or anything that looks remotely dangerous. Oh, and STAY OUT of that cupboard with the giant WARNING sign on it, understood?'

We all nodded vigorously. I had a suspicion any wrong-doers were going to ignore her advice entirely.

She continued. 'I'll also be your drama teacher. Yes, that's right, I'm a drama teacher with a chemistry lab. Make all the jokes you want; I've heard them all.'

Conor turned to me before she could even finish her sentence, his face filled with giddy excitement. 'What do you think? Something about Romeo and Juliet having "explosive chemistry",' he mused.

I stifled my laughter. He stared at me intently, clearly waiting for my contribution.

I racked my brain, desperately trying to think of something funny. It was so unfair—I could usually make hilarious jokes when I wasn't under pressure.

Have you got something? I asked Phobos.

'No. You're not funny,' they harshly reminded me.

Instead, I decided to say nothing and pretended to look interested in my blank notebook.

Mrs Shaxley went over the register again. 'Mr Barnaby, absent,' she murmured under her breath. I wanted to raise my hand, tell her I was here, but nerves got the better of me. I stayed silent; I'd rather get punished for skipping school than speak up in front of the class.

'Hey, Mrs Shaxley, Will's here,' Conor said, pointing at me.

I turned a little red, but more than that, I was surprised he spoke up for me.

'Oh'—she looked up—'well, say something next time.' Very useful advice.

www.ingramcontent.com/pod-product-compliance
Lightning Source LLC
Chambersburg PA
CBHW071855020426
42331CB00010B/2520